Golden Epoch-
The Last Stride

Golden Epoch-
The Last Stride

Vikramjeet Singh

Rajarshi Publications

Nagbani Road, Jammu

Rajarshi Publications
Nagbani Road, Jammu

First Edition, 2024
Price: Rs.199.00
© Copyright, 2024, Author

INDEX

14. The law of attraction revisited
15. Mismatch between the mental self and the ideal self
16. Higher Purpose in Life
17. Do Karmas need to be blamed?
18. Always try to be the best version of yourself.
19. Meeting the Ends of Life
      (a) Goal of life

1. Introduction to Brahman

This whole world is the essence of Brahm (Atma). Everything that is depicted here is just a reflection of that supreme reality. Those who are ignorant attach themselves to the reflection. Those who are seers understand their divine connection, merge with divine consciousness, and become observers. Every aspect of the outside world is subject to change. Thus, people who fix their minds on any external aspect remain oblivious to divine reality. For understanding our divine connection, all the worldly knowledge that is acquired needs to be forgotten. This is possible only when the mind is overpowered by Spirit and can be easily achievable through regular enchanting of Aum in a scientific manner. By doing this, faculties of mind seize their operations, and when all clouds created by delusion evaporate, only then can one immerse in its source and see its actual position as Brahm. This transcendental state of supreme absolute truth, or Brahm, is variously defined by the use of the words Om Tat Sat and also by the words Sat Chit Anand. However, the emphasis always remains to depict consciousness, bliss, and absolute truth.

To understand this core concept, the story of Ribhu and Nidhaga as narrated in Vishnu Puran needs a special mention here.

There was a great sage in our tradition whose name was

Ribhu Maharishi. He had one disciple whose name was Nidhaga. Ribhu Maharishi had a great affection for him, though he was not as focused as that of others. And that love was obviously due to the purity of his heart.

One day, Ribhu Maharishi disguised himself as a village rustic and went where Nidhaga was. A king's procession was passing by on the street. Nidhaga was watching the procession so enthusiastically. So Ribhu Maharishi went and stood near him and asked,What are you looking at?"?

Nidhaga thought to himself, "Everybody is looking at the procession. This fool doesn't know what we are looking at."

He said, "I am looking at the king's procession."

Village rustic asked,Where is the king?

"Can't you see? He's sitting on the elephant," Nidhaga replied.

The village rustic again asked, "Which one is the king?"

Now Nidhaga got angry and said, Can't you see? The man who is sitting above is the king; the animal below is the elephant."

So the villager again questioned, "What is the above and below? I don't understand."

On this Nidhaga became really angry and said, "Don't you know what is above and below?

So in order to give the villager a befitting reply, Nidhaga

told the villager to sit, and he himself stood on his shoulders. "And said, Now you can understand? Now me, who is standing upon you, is above, and you, who is lying down, is below.

On this, the village rustic again said that now he does not understand, but what is this you and me?

Suddenly the basic question of you and me both is Brahm struck Nidhaga. He felt at Ribhus feet as he realised that this villager was indeed his master. Thus Nidhaga learnt his final lesson on ultimate reality.

When life is governed by our base nature or instincts, then we remain ignorant about our true selves and remain oblivious to reality. This way, we also unconsciously create impediments in our lives. However, these hurdles automatically dissipate when we acquire true knowledge of Brahman. We cannot evade the effects of past deeds but can rework upon ourselves so that we may not indulge in nescience any further.

In reality, there is some higher spirit or almighty guiding our way. Without its supreme will, even a particle cannot move. So without its permission, nothing happens. It is indeed the prime causal force that works purely on the universal principle of truth. When our lives are attuned with truth, it protects us and fulfils all our needs. However, when we deviate from the path of truth, the seeds of negative karma, in the form of cause and its effect, get embedded into our psyche. In this scenario, the truth still prevails, but we get derailed and covered by illusion. Owing to

misinterpretation, the mind thinks that it would be able to direct the outcome of his actions or control what will happen to it. However, time never allows it to cross the barrier imposed by karma and vice versa, and this vicious cycle keeps rotating until the mind obeys the universal laws. Thus our own ignorance leads us to be enmeshed in endless cycles of birth and rebirth, pleasure and sorrows, meeting and parting, and the likewise, which also leads to the waywardness of mind. Still, the mind seldom realises its fundamental mistake and remains entrapped in its own cocoon of karmas. When the mind ultimately surrenders to the prime cause or Almighty and starts flowing with it, then it gives light to the truth, which ultimately leads to eternal bliss. In the given scenario, the mind reflects the spirit of Almighty, which we then call the soul, and its essence is Sat (truth), Chit (consciousness), and Anand (bliss). When this mind turns into a universal mind or pure consciousness, it becomes the part and parcel of the almighty. In this regard, after getting realisation of self, nature follows all its commands and obeys them, as nature is nothing but the consort or power of self or soul. Then whatever is uttered becomes truth, reflected becomes enlightening, and embraced becomes blissful.

2. The last stride

When everything was looking perfect and it seemed that life had gained its value and there was only one single leap left to touch the sky, suddenly everything started shaking and all life started to shatter with a small blow of wind. Some power indeed showed its presence. There was some fundamental mistake that took all life away. In the stride for excellence, there had been sprouted the seeds of ignorance, which had created a false identity. Now there were only two options left—either to accept the false identity and prosper in seeds of illusion or to set alight one's own shadow and enlighten the path in search of truth. The latter was chosen, and that was the last stride.

Throughout our lives, we try to satiate the desires arising in one's mind, and while fulfilling such desires, we make our mind so powerful that it creates our separate identity based upon such desires. As we enmesh into mental jugglery, we lost our true identity, and this way we would never be able to surrender before our true nature, viz., self, which indeed is the source of all attraction and from which emanates all eternal joy and bliss.

Essentially, it is the trivial_nature of the mind that whenever it gets attracted to something, then it generates thoughts related to it. Thereafter it multiplies such thought to its multifold and thus never seizes its action till a certain force, either internal or external, is applied upon it. It is pertinent to mention here that there are four constituents of mind, viz., Manas, Buddhi, Ahamkara, and Chitta. These together are called Antahkaran, which means inner instruments or organs. In the Manas resides all the thoughts—well planned and imaginative (Sankalp Vikalp); in the Buddhi resides all decisions or determinations (Nishchaye); in chitta all the impressions, memories, and past experiences are stored (Smriti or chintan); and in Ahamkar resides identification or attachment with the gross body or individuality (Aham or ego). Thus, all these instruments operate incessantly and deprive us of true knowledge of self.

Our past karmic flow conditions the state of our mind, and we indulge in certain thoughts or activities repeatedly and unconsciously because of strong karmic imprints ingrained in our minds. It is from the flow of these thoughts that the mind indeed survives itself and receives constant joy or sorrow based upon positive and negative karma. Essentially, one has to learn the right course of action so that it may not create negative karma in its basket due to wrong mental conditioning. By creating a vicious cycle of negative karma, we not only create hurdles in our lives but also disturb the living world around us due to interactional forces. It is thus very necessary for the mind to flow in the right direction so that the work of survival of nature vis-à-vis. fulfilling one's personal needs could be best established. This indeed is the work of establishing the Dharma, or righteousness, that survives mankind and all other creations.

Further, as illuminated in the Vedas, the dharma rests on

four pillars. Truth (Satya), Austerity (Tapas), Compassion (Karuna), and Charity (Daan) (where the latter also gives way to the former). Thus, it is prudent to check the flow of mind through regular contemplation based upon the above-mentioned pillars of righteousness. However, this marvel can only be fully achieved when the mind, after burning all past karmas, rests at its exalted state, i.e., Trikuti (Centre of Forehead), where it is fully conscious, and in the light of true knowledge, it acts to establish universal peace and harmony.

It is prudent to mention here that the Vedantins (those who follow the Vedas or secret knowledge of self) talk about cosmic order or Rita, which no one can surpass. Even Gods can't violate this universal order, which is based on truth. In this regard, when someone doesn't follow this order, he spreads anarchy and works opposite to the forces of nature that establish life. It is at this juncture that the divine interferes and punishes the person who is creating chaos and disturbance in the otherwise smooth functioning of nature. Even the persons who support the evil designs of such a wrong person, notwithstanding whether they are right or wrong on their own, indeed give power and strength to such faulty actions against the divine. Thus, a person who supports the ill cause also suffers the ill effects generated by such faulty actions.

Life is indeed the outcome of certain patterns of consciousness. When anyone disturbs the healthy conditions of life, it works against life. It is the prime objective of the divine to establish righteousness and thereby fight the sinister designs of evil. The epics like Ramayana and Mahabharata are live examples that explain the victory of truth over evil, the good being, the forces that support nature's cause or truth, and vice versa. Thus one should always remain conscious about such aspects while performing their actions and never get swayed by blindly following or supporting the wrong deeds, as our sole purpose in life is to establish dharma or righteousness, which in turn connects us with who we truly are.

Fundamentally, the true nature of self is based upon righteousness. When one performs his deeds based upon righteousness, then he starts dwelling within and gets acquainted with one's true self. Thus one's last stride is to surrender before the truth and merge within one's true self rather than solely living in duality created by the mind. The more the person indulges in the objects created by the mind, the farther they are from one's true self.

3. We are already encrypted to follow the truth.

Truth is our sublime nature, which works on the principle of oneness of being, or Advaita. When all the sheaths of ignorance are removed, then what remains is pure consciousness and a blissful state of truth, which the Vedantins called Brahm or Brahman. Our real self corresponds to our inner being (or inner voice), which is based upon truth and whose essence is Sat Chit Anand. Essentially, we are not a body of five elements but are part and parcel of divine reality. Only because we distract from our real nature, i.e., the truth, do we start leading an illusory life and become entrapped in it. As we move towards the truth, we start feeling blissful and get in tune with our real selves.

Truth is the eternal law of nature from which all other universal laws take their root. The universal laws are oneness of being, the immortality of the soul, the law of austerity or tapas, the law of karma or action, the law of devotion or attraction (depending upon one's intention), knowledge of self for liberation, the law of inertia or limited energy, the law of conservation of energy or consciousness, Individuality has to give way to universality, the establishment of Dharma, Forgiveness and nonattachment lead to expansion of being, eternal blissful nature of the soul, creation of mind based upon desires and their multiplication, and completeness of being or self-actualisation, consciousness and its ignorance can't reside together. Positivity and negativity both come from nature and are the essence of God. Love for creation leads to self-growth and vice versa, etc., and the final being the truth, which qualifies all the universal laws.

As already discussed, Dharma, or righteousness, rests on 4 pillars. The first and foremost pillar of dharma is truth. This is the basic fundamental principle that is reflected in the form of a supreme consciousness state, or Advaita. The whole world emanates from one single word, i.e., Shabd Brahm, or universal consciousness sound. Truth is synchronous with this supreme reality and is a foundational pillar for all subsequent creations. All life rests on this principle, and there can be no life possible devoid of truth. Truth indeed is the essence of all creation. Satya yuga is marked by the presence of truth and is the guiding force behind all knowledge and actions.

As the consciousness of the Supreme Being splits into multifold dimensions, the awareness related to it also disperses. Here all the dimensions have their own understanding of where nature or sound energy in the form of cosmic intelligence works for the survival of life. Here the word (Shabd Brahm) turns into a world that gives new dimensions of love, light, and life to it. Where there is a seed of creation or life, the same sound energy is called Brahma; where there is love and nourishment, the sound energy is called Vishnu; where there is discernment between right and wrong, the same energy is called Shiva; and to grow in this understanding, one needs to direct all energy and consciousness towards realising each dimension of life and ultimately the truth. The phenomenon, which is called tapas or austerity, takes place at this stage, which is synchronous with our concentration or focus to understand our ideal nature. The more austerities the person performs, the more it becomes conscious of reality. However, for performing austerities, a person first needs to develop his body and psyche so that they become capable of withstand the fire of knowledge within. This leads to the foundation of Treat Yuga, which finds its basis on the pillar of tapas, or austerity.

As the consciousness splits further, it leads to the creation of a false identity based upon duality. However, the people or individual beings who may be incarnated still belong to each other and help each other to realise their full potential. This feeling of togetherness and helping each other to resolve problems in their lives is the feeling of compassion, which is the purest form of love and unites each one by their source or with the divine. Thus this pillar of compassion or eternal love leads to the foundation of Dwapar yuga. This is the stage of duality with an inherent feeling of oneness.

In the kali yuga, this consciousness of oneness goes to an abysmal low. Here the individuality partakes to its grossest level. The consciousness of being gets struck to annamaya kosha. In simpler terms, a person gets confined to one's physical body only, forgetting his divine link with the cosmos. This stage is marked highly by the presence of ignorance and illusions, which bind all beings from exploring their inner divine nature. There are many reasons for getting entrapped in an illusory life. The major is an attachment to what is around us, which is synchronous to our time. The other thing is the fear of losing one's identity, which indeed is false and misleading. At this stage, righteousness or dharma can be realised through the medium of offerings or charity to others. This way, the person can delve inside one's self through the law of karma. Selfless Offerings (Nishkam Bhav) to others would help to reunite with one's self as the right deeds performed even devoid of true knowledge finally lead one to the knowledge of self through the law of reverse action or the law of karma or action.

These are stages of the level of consciousness based upon righteousness. At each stage, there is a level of understanding about universal laws. Each level is a creation, and every creation is complete in itself and is based upon a certain level of consciousness and intelligence. **It is pertinent to mention here that every level, when accomplished, becomes the basis for the next level, where one transforms or gives way to another until an absolute state of oneness or truth is reached**. Pertinent to mention here that truth is latently embedded in each pillar of righteousness. Without truth, no stage of consciousness qualifies to understand the essence of reality.

Thus, when we are on the path of truth, there is not much to lose but everything to gain. What we have to lose are our misconceptions, our wrong ideals, our faulty habits, our deteriorated consciousness level, and our sole bondage on knowledge gained only through the five sense organs. On the

Contrary to what we gain is belief in ourselves, higher control over our lives, and identifying with our real self, which is the source of eternal bliss or happiness, and most importantly, our sense of unity with the whole cosmos, whose indivisible part we are.

When we are distracted from the path of truth, then we create a web of karmas around us related to our instant understanding of things. Due to a lack of complete understanding, we also easily become prey to misconceptions, which further lead to the sprouting of wrong karmas in our basket. This, in turn, causes a vacuum in certain aspects of life due to the wrong channelisation of energy and forms a dwelling place for certain vikaras. Thus we may reap the ill effects of negative karmas together with other shortcomings in the form of vikaras. So in a way, we can't escape ourselves till we do not have the right understanding of things and correct the faulty karma that lies at its base. So to get out of this vicious cycle of illusion and ignorance, we need to first neutralise the wrong karmas that have taken root and have caused the creation of invisible knots in our lives. Pertinent to mention here that Vedas also talk about three knots, or Granthis, that tie us to ignorance, viz., Brahma Granthi, Vishnu Granthi, and Rudra Granthi. Here Brahma granthi (the knot of creation) holds us to mooladhar chakra and Swadhisthan chakra—the chakras associated with physical plane; Vishnu granthi (the knot of preservation) limits our consciousness further from Manipura till Anahat chakra—the chakras associated with subtle plane; and Rudra granthi (the knot of destruction) binds us from Anahat up to vishuddhi chakra and ajna chakra—the chakras correspond to the causal plane. Only when we untie our consciousness from these knots of illusion do we understand ourselves fully.

4. Need to reroute Mind

We have deviated from our true nature. We have complicated our lives and created clouds of illusion and ignorance around us. We have created a cobweb of superstitious beliefs and unrealistic ideas. Not only to this, but we have well-kept all such thoughts under an envelope created by our ego. This creates our separate identity from others or deviates us from the ultimate. We are so attached to this identity that if anybody tries to enter our forewall, then it seems to impose a threat upon us. Thus, if we see anybody is inflicting harm to our ego or limited self, then we retaliate in anger and also become ready to kill or die to protect our wrong or unrealistic notions. We never let reason or rationale come across, which may challenge our wrong notions and unrealistic beliefs. So no one except us can ever help us to proceed to our real abode, i.e., truth, where the supreme consciousness dwells. Thus nobody except ourselves can be our real saviour, which helps us to sail through life.

When the mind surrenders all its actions to the divine and tries to observe the divine pattern within, then slowly and steadily it starts submerging into divinity, where an individual mind that is limited to needs created by bodily senses transforms into a universal mind based upon universal principles and ultimately to the soul, where it receives wisdom from the universe. All this happens automatically, as our true nature is divine, which we forget due to the overshadowing of real selves with ignorance and illusion. Further, till the mind concentrates only upon certain aspects of reality and compromises the whole, there remains duality, and it cannot become one with the divinity or soul residing within. So our real self remains out of our reach till all instruments of mind, viz. Aham, Chitta, Manas, and Buddhi, seize all their operations and surrender before the whole of our being. In the later chapters, when we study the concept of Vaishvanara Atma, we will understand that the whole cannot be understood through partitioning. However, we cannot realise our whole being without first realising all aspects of the divine. For this, we need to return to our inherent nature and thoroughly understand different aspects of life after delving within. Only after having a complete understanding of our being vis-à-vis the laws of nature governing life can we expand our consciousness and energy aura to fully realise ourselves. Further, for complete understanding, we must be free from all operations of mind and instead start observing their patterns and mechanisms. We can know about their mechanisms fully when we separate ourselves from all actions of the mind, viz., thoughts, emotions, conceptions, etc. **A soul is a witness entity that is free from all operations of the mind and thus can never be known but can only be experienced.**

When we channel our mind based upon our inner self (corresponding to our inner divine voice), then it drives the mind to the path of enlightenment or truth. However, before real surrender, we must be acquainted with all aspects of reality, which is possible only when the mind is free from all kinds of vikaras. Further, while treading the path of enlightenment, the mind only has a limited understanding of reality based on its present consciousness level. Thus the mind has either to depend upon a realised soul or on one's self (inner light or knowledge) to reach its true destination, which reflects itself in the form of inner proclivity. Many people are not able to strive for this transformation of mind because on this path we are required to shed our limited ego and surrender completely before truth or onto our soul. It also requires the development of the mind from one conscious level to another till a level of oneness, or Advaita, is not reached. Till then, we always encounter ignorance in one form or another. At each level, we need to shed our limited identity and adopt higher principles of life. The mind, being the outcome of certain aspects of consciousness and corresponding intellect, tries to resist every attempt to change and must be guided adequately by one's higher intellect vis-à-vis the soul. Wherever the mind agitates or gets disturbed, the journey comes to a standstill, and till it is not motivated again, the self remains constrained despite knowing the reality. With ignorance of mind and actions that follow as a result, the negative karmic forces again come into play, which further binds the mind to ignorance and illusion. In such a scenario, we would require bearing the ill effect of negative karma before taking a re-course to ourselves. Thus, a right understanding of mind or consciousness is a prerequisite before treading the spiritual path.

To fulfill our life's purpose and to reach our true destination, we should remain clinging to truth in all facets of life. When we follow the path of truth, we keep getting guidance and protection from the divine. However, if for any reason we deviate from the path, then that cause starts to attract us infinitely, and thus we forget about our actual path and remain possessed by it until our self or inner consciousness does not intervene our way. But this causes much harm to our psyche. Thus we must always remain conscious as well as surrender to the universal spirit so that we continue to receive divine grace. Anything that seems to compromise our consciousness or our mind should never be followed, irrespective of how small it seems at first glance. If we follow the truth, then it becomes the responsibility of the truth or universal laws to protect us, but if we deviate from the truth, then nobody will be our saviour, and we will have to repent such deeds sooner or later, and it would also degrade our mind. In this regard, it has to be understood that we are not the body of five elements or a mind or intellect, but these are only serving our purpose, and we are the essence of divinity, which reflects itself in the form of truth or universal order. Thus, truth should be followed in all given circumstances to realise one's true self.

In this journey of mind, the enchanting of Aum is of paramount importance. Aum's vibrations attract the mind (which is struck in Mooladhara chakra) to enter the Sushmana canal (that flows inside the backbone), and through its upward trend leads the mind in its upward journey, which finally settles at Trikuti chakra and there by having a complete understanding of all aspects of life vis-à-vis nourishing all the spiritual centres. Further, **by attaining a complete understanding of life, we become aware of our faults. and,**

with the grace received from the Almighty, can work to replace them with the correct ones. Further, as we feed ourselves with higher vibrations through regular enchanting of aum as well as by following the path of truth, our inner self would automatically become predominant and take hold of our life. Pertinent to mention here that our self is the essence of divine reality, which has become dormant due to incessant action of the mind. Further, when this self of ours is realised, after peeling off all layers of ignorance, then it acts to establish truth and thereby experience its inherent divine nature of eternal bliss and peace. Further, it becomes able to direct the mind and thus channel it to make tuning with universal laws.

Till we do not adhere to universal principles, we cannot move even an inch towards reality. Even if somehow we manage to make a temporary halt at the higher dimension of life based upon certain conditioned behaviour, even then our lack of complete understanding keeps disturbing our peace of mind and, in turn, causes one or other vikara to predominate our lives. To balance all aspects, we need to adopt the appropriate behaviour and thinking pattern most conducive to creating better karmas in tune with universal laws. Thus, for the realisation of self, one must try to raise the level of consciousness and should also try to understand the art of balancing all the aspects of life through careful thought and followed by the right behaviour. When our mind gets fully attuned to universal laws, then it merges into the self. Here, the self turns into a soul and thereby embarks on the most sacred journey of God realisation.

5. We have lost the true direction of life.

It seems that nobody bothers about their true destination. Everybody does their work only to sustain their perishable body without acknowledging the purpose of their coming into being. We have started thinking of ourselves as mortals and thus remain at the mercy of time and circumstances for our very survival. On the contrary, our forefathers used to live in consonance with nature. They had indeed realised themselves to be souls or part and parcel of the divine spirit. They were not over-attached to their body or the objects of senses, and thus they would also never surpass the laws of nature. Thus they had close connectivity with divinity and the divine plan and would continue to receive the divine grace in the form of infinite bliss. Due to this, they had developed complete control over themselves. They also realised that they had themselves wear this perishable body and would leave their body at their own will to serve some higher purpose. Thus they were liberated souls and had developed authority over time and would themselves decide what would happen to them.

Due to over-identification with our body now a days, **we never try to delve within and listen to our inner divine sound, which unites us with our true self, which is truth.** Again, it has been seen that many of us know about the truth,

But out of fear of losing something unknown, we keep saying that we would devote time to realise ourselves after a certain amount of time would elapse or after crossing such and such age. How foolish we are that we even think that we need a certain time to get acquainted with our true selves. In actuality, the thing is that we are so attached to our perishable bodies and to our near and dear ones that we have some illusionary fear of losing them if we tread the inner divine path. Due to overly attachment, we flout universal laws many times, which causes a vicious karmic circle to be created around us, which then never lets us unify with our divine nature. On the contrary, with time this attachment would not cease but become deeper and deeper, and after some time it becomes our identity itself, from which we would never be able to separate ourselves no matter how hard we try. Moreover, untie from the knot of attachment and illusion is a long process as it requires us to reframe our karmas based upon truth so that they may liberate us from all types of bondages. This process demands our steadiness and persistence, not our speed. Apt to mention here that setting aside attachment does not mean we seize to love our body or those to whom we relate. Nor does it mean to corner from our roles and duties. It simply means that we channel our minds to focus on understanding the deep mysteries of life and streamline our lives to live a more fulfilling life after its proper channelization. Have we ever tried to do justification with all dimensions of life, viz., physical, mental, intellectual, and spiritual? If not, now is the right time to do it. Till the mind is attached to neuroscience, it cannot function fully to realise its true potential. However, when it starts to shatter the layers of illusion and delusions, only then does it become one with the cosmos and divine plan.

Since the mind has indulged more in outer reality, it always tries to possess all material endowments in a lesser time. So it tries to hanker after everything outwardly, and while attaining things, it tries to work on the principle of speed. It thinks that the faster it functions, the better it is. We also try to work on that speed. In that matter, everybody is in the race and tries to catch up with the time. But one thing to understand is that with more speed we become more involved in the gross world, and with this, we remain oblivious about subtle aspects of life for which we are required to surrender and thereby observe the true nature of our being. By indulging more in outer aspects only, we also kill creativity and spiritual prospects within. However, despite our ignorance inflicting much harm on us, we seldom apply the faculties of our minds to understand reality.

In the given context, **it has also been observed that the individual mind functions on possibilities, whereas nature functions on universal laws**. So whenever we create certain possibilities in life, the mind starts functioning over them infinitely and comes up with altogether different scenarios to express our lives. Not only this, but it also attracts likewise frequencies, which then occupy a deeper space in our mind and thus also govern our intellect. Thus, to understand reality, we are required to surrender ourselves to cosmic force and then analyse things in the light of true knowledge. We have to become silent in our minds to catch up with the time. We can understand the time dimension only when we stop running and start observing how our body, or for that matter, how this universe is functioning, and streamline our lives accordingly. We need to surrender all thoughts and preconceived ideas to understand reality. **Till the mind is attached to so many things, it never stops its action and thus remains engaged in it all the time and thus could never be able to grasp the reality of things**. Only when we devote time for ourselves that the true knowledge sprouts from within, and by following the right course of action in our life, we will be able to achieve our true destination vis-à-vis raising our consciousness with each passing day.

To understand reality, we need to challenge every existing thought or preconceived idea and test it in the light of truth. Only when it passes the test of time should it be inculcated in our lives. Anything that deviates us from the path of truth should either be cornered from our life at once or else be tried to streamline in light of truth.

Now somebody asks if the deities and other idols whom we worship from the core of our mind are different from the almighty or universal truth. In that case, suppose you are working in an organisation. Now answer: that would you treat your immediate senior equivalent to the head of the organisation?   No doubt we should venerate all our seniors and obey them; however, the head of the organisation should not be forgotten, as he is the main force behind all. Likewise, we should respect and may take blessings from all higher creations, but during the process, we should not break our connection with the creator, who itself is beyond all names and forms, yet all the creation is part and parcel of divine (Param-atma) and expresses the divine only. And if we forget the divine in between, then we have indeed forgotten our very source from which we have taken root and unto whom we finally have to take a halt. Again, cosmic divine force is the supreme controller of all creation, and it is only with its divine will that the whole universe gains momentum. Thus, it only decides what would happen to us and how we live our lives. Even the grace we receive from the deities is indeed the grace received from Almighty God.

Apt to mention here that notwithstanding the universal laws, everybody has their own consciousness and energy level, so we have our own. Further, **one must also understand that energy flows with the pattern of our consciousness. Thus, when we align our consciousness with universal laws, then the right or universal energy will always follow.** Moreover, our consciousness is guided by our intentions, which in turn define our proclivity towards life. Thus, it is our prime duty to raise our consciousness so that we can move towards the ultimate reality in due course.

Everybody works as per level of their understanding, and as we step up from our existing levels, we come closer to the universal plan. It has to be understood that we all have emanated from the same source, but due to forces of illusion,

We have enveloped ourselves with ignorance. Spirituality is peeling off these layers of ignorance and seeing ourselves as a soul. These layers are bodily senses, prana, mind, intellect, and finally the subtlest being the individual self, which has to turn into the universal self or soul. However, this is possible only through correct understanding and realisation of our true potential. So inside all of us, there is a capacity to realise the self, which is independent of all genotypes and phenotypes that we inherit through genes. However, we are so engrossed in this mental jugglery or mundane aspects of the outer world that we rarely dwell within and listen to our inner voice.

There is a story to understand the effect of a little deviation on life's path and the envelope of illusion. One day, while wandering on earth, Sage Narada asked Vishnu Ji why the people on earth could not spare much time for their worship, as you are the benefactor of all. To this lord replied that due to Maya (illusion), the world remains engrossed in different objects and thus could rarely come to me. Narada further showed his desire to get acquainted with this Maya, which envelops the minds of all the creation. On seeing such confusion on the face of Narada, Lord told him, Can you bring me a little water in your water pot (kamandal) from the nearby water source as he is feeling thirsty? At the request of the lord, Narada went to take water from river water. As he was taking water, he saw a maiden woman who had flawless beauty. On seeing her, Narada starts to embrace the beauty that has been bestowed upon her by the Lord. The lady seeing Narada ji paid venerations to him and invited him to their house out of utter respect. Narada Ji also accepted the request and accompanied her to their house. On seeing Narada ji in their house, the parents of the lady felt blessed and also offered the Narada ji to stay there and marry their maiden girl. On this Narada ji thought that he had every knowledge of the world except the life of a household, and it is also necessary to experience this phase of life as well. So, Narada Ji also accepted the offer and started to dwell there. Many years passed, and Narad Ji was deeply engrossed in family chores. Narad ji also had children, and he got attached to this life. Everything was going smoothly when one day there was a flood in their village. Everything washed with it. His children, wife, house, and everything drowned. Narada Ji could only be able to save his own life and was crying bitterly. While he was in great remorse, he heard a meek voice from a distant place asking Narada Ji to bring drinking water. At first, he tried to ignore the voice, but with time it became louder, and when he tried to search for the person who was making this voice, he saw the lord waiting for Narada Ji, and with this, all the scenes of the flood and everything instantly disappeared, and now only the lord and Naradji remained. Realising the effect of Maya had taken place, the Naradji fell into the feet of the Lord and showered his gratitude for always being his saviour.

Our life is like a quagmire that has captivated our being, and we cannot help ourselves to get out of it. Life attracts us towards outside charm, which is only a shadow of reality. We experience life through bodily senses and mind and also through our limited intellect borne out of knowledge attained by senses and mind. Thus we cannot see the truth as it is and remain engrossed in this Prapancca (world) created by sense organs and mind. Only when we surrender our will to the almighty will it take us out of this quagmire, and thus we can realise ourselves to be the essence of the almighty. The best way to unite with divinity is through regular enchanting of aum, which leads the mind to its exalted state. Only after the mind reaches its exalted state can we understand our relationship with the almighty and can completely surrender before the divine to understand the truth. So, regular enchanting of aum acts as a rope that would render support to us and would not let us sink if we held it tight, as it connects us with supreme reality or the almighty. It also helps us realise our full potential, viz., bodily, mental, intellectual, and spiritual, and also makes us the lord of three worlds, viz., the physical, mental, and spiritual realms, from merely living a minuscule or very limited life. Pertinent to mention here that for full realisation, our body should also be required to function optimally and adapt to the better ways of life, thus also overcoming the challenges imposed by our genes as well as our environment. **Thus, complete realisation also encapsulates the realisation of the full potential of the body, mind, and soul.**

6. Getting introduced to reality

We can never find satisfaction till we are estranged from our real selves, whose essence is Sat Chit Anand. All the material endowments and relations are short-lived and provide us only momentary relief. We experience real satisfaction when we return to our true nature. Till we are attached, we cannot live freely, and till our life and energy are not attuned with natural/universal laws, there can't be any mental peace as well as equilibrium in life.

To understand the last stride, we come across the story of three friends, namely Ramesh, Lokesh, and Sukhnandan. According to their temperaments, Ramesh was witty and would try to find out the reason behind everything and was hard-working, optimistic, and would embrace very high ideals in life. Lokesh was a brilliant student from the very beginning. He had a strong grasp of things and had to do with understanding the various complexities of life. Moreover, he believed in action and would thus remain engaged in several pursuits that he decided for himself. However, he doesn't indulge in higher ideals and would work only to make his life comfortable and at ease. On the contrary, Sukhnandan had a fun-loving personality, knew the art of going well along with others, and was a very devoted person. As per his temperament, he looked for joy and happiness in his work and would work to make his life comfortable and joyful.

As fate decided it, all three became acquaintances with each other in due course of time. Ramesh faced many struggles and challenges in life as he had to start from scratch. It would seem that problems had such great companionship with Ramesh that they never left him alone, even for a single moment. Where everybody settled in their lives, Ramesh would remain meshed up with one thing or the other. He would seem to be starting many new projects, however, not settling at any place and would only swing from one place to another. Lokesh used to make fun of Ramesh for not settling and always changing his mind now and then. Whereas Lokesh took expertise in one or more skills based on his proficiency and started to boom in those fields. Sukhnandan had his own plans, and he always looked at fun while doing things.

With time, Ramesh started to have thorough knowledge and expertise over things, and his attitude of striving for knowledge opened the door to many possibilities before him. He preferred to choose the wisest course, and he became a renowned philosopher and a writer, for his theories had earned a lot of respect among large masses. Finally, his inquisitive nature and his faith in the Almighty took him to the journey of self. Lokesh owned many businesses, including health centres, restaurants, gossip zones, etc. He remained grounded yet ambitious, and because of his strong inclination towards a healthy life, he made a strong basis for life to flourish. Indeed, he became successful in all his endeavours and excelled a lot in terms of health and material prosperity. Besides, Sukhnandan became a renowned artist. He opened art schools and restaurants and also became a public speaker.

However, all three were excelling in their fields, yet they were not living beside each other for a long time. So one day they decided to meet and spend some quality time and embrace their reunion. At the meeting, everybody narrated their own success stories. However, Ramesh had a great change in his personality and behaviour. He had become more grounded and high-spirited than ever. On noticing this, Lokesh and Sukhnandan got amazed. Lokesh asked Ramesh, Have you got a certain hidden treasure or that you have lost your senses due to the overburden of life? Now, Ramesh gently gave a smile and told him that all these years he has tried to learn the true significance of life, and he is rather living a more fulfilled life after resorting to his inner sublime nature. Looking at his polite gesture, Lokesh and Sukhnandan became curious to know more about the same and asked for it. To this, Ramesh replied that you can't understand my point of view till you are not well versed with life and its real purpose. Even before I may tell you about the true mantra of life, I would like to throw some light on the body and Vikaras that captivate mind and intellect in their stranglehold and which in turn restrict the mind to engage in free inquiry and thereby realise its full potential.

a) Body and Vikaras

Our body is primarily composed of five elements, and disturbance to any of these elements leads to the emergence of disorder in the body, which we then called vikara. There are five major vikaras or vices, viz. Kama (lust), Krodh (anger), Lobh (greed), Moh (attachment), and Ahankar (pride or ego).

that loot the consciousness and energy of the person when they are unchecked. However, when properly regulated by the mind, they become their true friends. They are to be effectively tackled before any spiritual attainments. The person who remains deeply indulged in any of such vikaras sooner or later becomes devoid of energy and vigour and also attracts and thereby indulges in other vikaras in due course of time. All the vikaras in true essence are the same, and the difference, if any, is only of appearance. These all vikaras emanate from excessive attachment to the body and to its sensual objects.

Life is properly established when we create a proper balance between all its aspects. An imbalance impedes our self-growth, and we may not be able to channel our energies to understand ourselves fully.   Thus, unregulated aspects of our lives create various imbalances or vikaras within us that require to be confronted and corrected before we tread any spiritual path. The chief Vikaras are Ahankar, Moh, Lobh, Krodh, and Kaam. Further, when energy in our body becomes dormant, it leads to another major vikara called Alasya. The detailed analysis of the ill effects of each Vikara is thoroughly discussed below:

Ahankar(Ego)

Ahankar, or ego, is that unregulated aspect of our lives where the mind creates its own separate identity based upon its values and thoughts. The problem arises when this ego is so deepened that we forget our true identity and lose our divine link with the cosmos. We try to preserve our false identity and, in the process, challenge and also counter the other facets of reality that are contradictory to our beliefs and faith. To the extent that we can also harm ourselves and others to keep this false identity alive. In this state, our lesser self (based upon ego) or individuality dances on the interplay of mind and nature and has to depend upon them for its survival. The right balance is struck when the mind realises its actual state, and thus, with the help of an enlightened mind, the self can realise its actual position as the soul. This soul is part and parcel of truth and is the controller of the whole cosmos and thus controls all aspects of life.

Till the mind does not start acting purely upon reason and logic, it continues to delve into the limited scope of life. Till then, it survives with its limited existence. When the mind finds its exalted state, then it also helps the self to find its real position, which thus turns into the soul, which is part and parcel of universal reality.

However, people try to keep their egos alive and forget their true divine nature. They try to preserve their thoughts and ideals at the cost of truth, and they take big vows and become limited to keep them alive. They are like Bhishampitama, Dronacharya, Karna, Ashwathama, etc., who, despite knowing reality, still follow the dictates of Duryodhana, or false identity, for one reason or another. They feed their egos day in and day out and make themselves very powerful by sticking to their notions. Pertinent to mention here that the stronger the thoughts, the more prevailing they become and, in turn, give a lot of energy to the person holding them. However, in the end, they cause equal pain when smeared a part by the blows of truth. These false ideals are required to be countered effectively by the mind, or Arjuna, under guidance received from one's soul, or Krishna.

Moh (Attachment)

The soul is part and parcel of the almighty, which is omnipresent. Due to bondage created by one's ego, we get entrapped in this body, where various forces of nature entangle us in its karmic flow. Due to overattachment, we disobey the universal laws to maintain proximity with the people or things that we embrace. Firstly, due to the attachment created by this body, we topple the universal laws to preserve this mortal body for long. It is here the mind comes into being, which creates its identity separate from the universal source. After having preserved the body, we next try to fulfil the desires and cravings that sprout from this body and, in turn, from the mind. We belong to certain objects and things and, as such, also develop strong bonds with them.

Overattachment restricts us from realising our potential fully. We engage ourselves in this body due to various desires and cravings sprouting out of our attachment. Thus, even if we have knowledge of the cosmos, we still choose to remain entangled in our self-cocoon in the hope to witness only the shadow of reality and to get happiness from momentary pleasure, which keeps with it a lot of miseries and sorrows afterwards. Nature is in constant flux, and the mind tries to keep things unchanged. It is where all struggle begins. Where we must flow with the natural pace and embrace things that come to us, we instead try to keep things aside and do not allow change to occur. However, when change occurs, we agitate and try to break down the natural laws and get entrapped in the cycle of karma by following wrong deeds.

Sometimes it so happens that when something dearest is taken away from us, then we lose trust in the universal spirit and become atheists. We deliberately break the laws to prove that irrespective of universal laws, we also have existence and that we would live it the way we want. We use our free will in a self-defeating way and get entrapped further into attachment with a lot of minor things in the form of addictions, which in turn binds us to karmic flow. Till we are not done away with every kind of attachment, there is every possibility that we fall prey to time. But when we let go of even the last object of our attachment, the time becomes irrelevant for us, as then we start to embrace the divinity in all of its forms. At that moment nature opens to us like a true friend and bestows us with every joy of life, as at this time we generally start to obey all laws of the cosmos and become part and parcel of omnipotent divine reality and thus develop Krishna consciousness, or simply become soul. Pertinent to mention here that **Krishna is regarded as a soul that loves all but attaches to none and also performs deeds tricking others on truth but always carries it and beholds it. However, Krishna, or soul, is itself the embodiment of truth and holds the whole of the universe within its selfless love and supreme sacrifice.**

Many learnt scholars know the reality very well but still become blind due to over-attachment, sometimes with their limited existence or sometimes for attachment to their loved ones. It has to be acknowledged, however, that a person cannot change the laws of nature, but by indulging in wrong deeds, he, along with others, would perish for breaking the universal laws. We perform misdeeds due to attachment and, due to this, forget our true selves, and later on, our ignorance about ourselves becomes the cause of all miseries. Thus attachment (Moh) has a direct link with illusion or ignorance (Maaya) and also the link that restricts our self-growth. To flow with nature and to embrace nature in all its forms is the key to all bliss and eternal peace.

Lobh (Greed)

Due to attachment to things, we try to accumulate more and more of them to satiate our being. We try to feed ourselves and those to which we are attached. We do this at the cost of those irrelevant to us. This greed becomes deeper and deeper as time passes, and no amount of wealth or material possessions can ever satiate that innate craving in us.

This happens because we expect these momentary things to give us eternal joy and prosperity. But when we miserably fail to satiate our inner being, then we become restless in pursuing our goals further and further, which in turn takes away all our peace and tranquilly of mind.

Tranquilly of mind is achieved when we are in harmony with our real nature. But as we deviate from our inner self and put more pressure on the mind to fulfil the outward things, then in a way we lose our way to harmonising all aspects of life, and instead our mind remains preoccupied with thoughts about accumulating more and more of something. We must understand that this something cannot be everything, and because we are oblivious to this reality, we never attain peace and harmony deep within.

We can see many people living their lives while craving more and more for material endowments. Even when nature has bestowed them with everything, their exaggerated desires never cease, and this makes them restless and unhappy with their lives. To the extent that they go to the extent of moral turpitude to which there is no forgiveness. The people resort to unscrupulous means to fulfil their desires, which may include graft, corruption, betraying their loved ones, harming people around them, abusing others, lying, killing, and the like. Thus, by indulging in such ill practices, they not only create obstacles for others but also make their lives hell by breeding wrong karmas for themselves.

We must live to satiate our being. Our mind should be focused on understanding the reality of things and taking recourse to self. It must behave proactively rather than instinctively. Our main focus should be to get acquainted with our real nature vis-à-vis. fulfilling the necessities of life. We must concentrate on ourselves so that we can understand the deep mysteries of life. We must meditate and collect hidden treasure that is lying deep within ourselves. The more we realise ourselves, the more happiness we start to experience within our lives. This outward greed naturally lessens as we get to know what is real and what is only momentary or unreal.

Krodh (Anger)

Anger is the expression of ego when desired things or states are not achieved adequately. Generally, when things do not happen as per expectation, a person feels frustrated and agitated. It is in this state that a person explodes and tries to harm the person responsible for it through any means possible. The expression of anger burns all the vital energy present in one's self and also kills the power to discern and make good judgement. Thus, it hurts more to oneself than to its recipient.

As already discussed, a person identifies himself with certain ideologies—either good or bad. Based upon this, it regulates one's conduct and that of others. Those who are more fanatic with their ideologies try to impose them upon others, and when they fail to do it, they generally resort to unscrupulous ways to dictate others, including the expression of anger.

People generally complain that they cannot overcome their anger, but deep inside they must understand that they indeed like their expression and are feeding it with their ego. So how can they overcome such wrong tendencies within themselves? One must understand that everybody has their ideologies in life, and we must accept them likewise. Our self should be such that it can accommodate and assimilate the others within oneself. True love pours when we accept the person with their flaws and try to nourish them in the best possible ways. In this regard, they must be welcomed with unconditional positive regard. However, sometimes, when people fail to understand your importance and rather continue to create hurdles in your life, it is prudent to keep them away for a while and till they do not understand the importance of one another in fulfilling the idea of life.

We may see many people who are most beautiful in their hearts, but all their beauty remains overshadowed, and they could not get along with others because of their anger. However, despite all the clues, they fail to understand that their overwhelmed anger is causing more instability in their life than causing momentary relief. Because of their exaggerated ego, they are unable to see the viewpoint of others and instead blame others for the folly befalling in their life. They should stop at once and look within themselves to get the answer to things. If they once settled down with their anger, then half of their problems would automatically subside, and they would see the all-new world full of fascination and hope.

Kaama (Lust)

Fire ignites the knowledge within us and keeps us liberated and united with ourselves. But when, due to anger or inertia, this fire cools down, it causes the unbridled flow of thoughts to creep, in which, when it takes a definite shape, is expressed in the form of lust. When we are unattached, we are liberated, but when we become overly attached and dipped, our psyche becomes entrapped by the source of our attraction. We can't escape our thoughts from certain objects that we crave and thus become overly possessive. Where the attraction is maximum, it is expressed in the form of lust. This Vikara cannot be overcome easily as it gets ingrained in our bodies and minds. We lose our focus and are engrossed in it fully. In simpler words, when we lose our consciousness or true focus and instead get hypnotised or charmed by the outer beauty of something or somebody, then we get distracted and, in turn, get lost. This is when we fall in love with the outer charm of life and forget about ourselves and the true purpose of our coming into being or our life. It becomes the biggest hurdle in the path of enlightenment if it is not tackled effectively. It comes into being when we are so charmed by the beauty of things that we forget to perform our allotted duty and lose focus from our goal. This vikara also has its roots in waywardness of mind. Thus it keeps circumventing around us in one form or another. Till we do not get into control of ourselves, it keeps haunting us and making us miserable at its hand.

Anything that is done under complete control of the mind and vis. a vis. obeying the universal laws that do not lead to the waywardness of the mind frees us from lust. Lust is encapsulated when the mind is corrupt and loses its focus on the objects of concentration. People often forget their roles and duties at the sight of something pleasant. The mind remains preoccupied, and a person craves certain situations to come across again and again. It also signifies an imbalance of the mind where it starts working on its own based upon instincts. It is an effective tool in the hands of negativity. It fills our minds with scrap matter, which distracts us from our life's goals. Pertinent to mention here that till the mind is entangled in its grip, it can't dwell effectively within self, and like a chemical reaction, it takes us away from our true self. The simplest way to tackle the lust is to never lose one's attention from oneself and never bind the mind at its hands. Once it takes control, it overshadows the intellect and consciousness. Like a turtle who contracts itself in the face of danger, a person who becomes fully engrossed in self at its face is truly ruled by self-commandments.

Once this vikara is controlled, we can focus on ourselves, which is like a luminous sun that otherwise remains shadowed or overpowered by the influence of clouds, which affects the psyche in the form of lust.

It has been observed that this lust, in whatever form, cannot be subdued completely until the independent presence of mind. However, when this aspect of life assimilates completely with the self, it becomes attuned with universal laws and can overcome all distractions caused by the creation of a false identity because the mind is aloof from the self.

Alasya (Laziness)

When the body lacks the requisite threshold energy to perform various activities, it resultantly causes inertia, which in turn restricts the mind from performing activity and thus keeps the energy or momentum of the body and mind to their minimum. Thus, people do not do things to improve their way of life and become tuned to their ill patterns of life. Even when they see sure success or improvement after performing a certain course of action or behaviour, they still choose to keep their energy in a resting state and make very little effort to cross the energy threshold as they become so attached to their routine based upon faulty behaviour due to inertia. They indeed either blame their fate for negative conditions of life or become overly dependent on their so-called destiny to improve their way of life. They indeed connect their success with destiny and their defeat with a lack of potential. They somehow resemble the psychological state of hypohedonia, where they cannot enjoy having success and, on the other hand, feel extremely remorseful and worthless at the hands of defeat.

When energy flows at its optimum level, there is cleanliness and discipline in life. The opposite is true when a person lacks it. Where there is cleanliness and order, the energy flows without constraint. Where there is disorder and chaos, the energy stuck in those points and could not flow freely and in unison with cosmic energy. The energy that gets stuck due to disorder and chaos is called entropy. This also led to obstruction in its free flow, which in turn caused inability or inertia to reach our full potential.

It is the biggest of all the Vikaras. It creates inertia in the body and mind, where they resist all the changes and rather remain in a dormant state. There is a requirement for extra energy to cross the threshold before doing any work. It is indeed the blockage created by the mind to realise or work up to its optimum capacity. Even if this threshold energy is possessed by the person, it makes bonhomie with this false state and tries to resist any attempt to change. This is the state of learnt helplessness. Even when obstacles from our path are removed, we prefer to stay there and blame our fate or karmas for negative life circumstances. Here we must learn to get out of such situations that cause inertia to prolong in our lives.

There is innate potential in us to actualise ourselves. There is an innate fire element in us that gives us the initial thrust to achieve various goals or cross the hurdles created in our lives. Due to anger, certain diseases, or certain other restrictions, this fire element gets disturbed, and when it is excessively consumed, it falls apart and we may slip downwards. In most ordinary terms, it overlaps with Tamas Guna, where the person remains at the base energy level and gets energy through sustaining the natural life cycle, viz., simply gaining energy through sleeping and eating without putting any efforts of one's own.

It can only be overcome when we take charge of our lives and perform activities to satiate the demands of our lives. It should be understood that with knowledge we can reach out to things, but to keep the things beside us, it should be followed by appropriate action. It has been noticed that when our energy aura vibrates at higher frequencies, then all inactivity or lethargy dissipates, which is only possible when backed by optimum activity. The more time we spend in activity, the more conscious we become, and the less we need leisure or sleep time to refresh ourselves because, at a higher level, we are more conscious beings than resting entities. In resting mode, there is more influence of nature, and at a higher level, there is more cosmic influence. Further, when we lay asleep, our mind ordinarily rests as per the pattern of our thoughts, which can be controlled and brought to higher consciousness at higher frequencies. Thus we must inculcate the habits of meditation, pranayama, physical exercises, and most importantly, walking to refresh our minds and overcome the seeds of inactivity in us, which only cause limited energy to flow within us and thus a low energy aura.

One more thing that has to be realised is that till we do not learn the right pattern of things, the energy within us remains stuck in one place or the other, which unconsciously restricts us from treading the inner pathways. The strong attraction towards things causes Raaga, or strong desire, and strong aversion to them causes dvesha (ill will), the two states that bind a mind to the samsaric wheel of incessant birth and death. Thus most important is the knowledge of all life phenomena, which, when lived in the right proportion followed by the right action with the right intention, leads us to become fully functional persons, thereby overcoming the threshold of nature. This becomes possible when we delve within, preferably through regular enchanting of Aum, and through understanding the play of sound and light—the twin basis of our very survival—we can understand our actual position vis-à-vis. gaining control over those subtle aspects of survival that are already explained here above.

(b) Relation between bodily senses and vikaras

All the knowledge of the outside world that we experience has become possible due to bodily senses, which include the senses of sight (fire), hearing (akasha), smell (earth), taste (water), and touch (air). These are called Tanmatras, and are indeed the essence or subtle aspects of Panch Mahabhutas, or five gross elements present in our body. When any of these elements or senses gets disturbed due to overindulgence, then it leads to vikara. They engulf the mind in its stranglehold and cause drainage of energy and consciousness. There is a need to control these vikaras by effectively regulating all of them optimally. They are like strings of the musical instrument, and when any one of them is disturbed (either too tight or loose), then it automatically disturbs the others. So great care is required so that a bodily balance is achieved. Further, when these are effectively regulated, then they become a boon to mankind. These are also the instruments of the body through which the mind interacts with nature or the outside world. They are essential for the survival of life on Earth. If there is no Kama, then the process of procreation ultimately stops; if there is no Krodh, then nobody would bother or care about another person as it is an expression of discontent; if there is no greed, then how can a person feed one's self and others; if there is no Moh or attachment, then how would a mother embrace and nourish and again, if there is no Ahamkar, then how would we be able to express our identity, and likewise, if there is no Alasya, then how would the body replenish its cells, and the body would get destroyed due to incessant work.

Thus, all these aspects are necessary for human survival, but they should be under proper watch and be well regulated. When the mind is overly indulged in them, then the consciousness cannot escape from it, and the mind cannot function upon higher aspects of life, viz., agility, love, compassion, sacrifice, etc. Lastly, due to consciousness being stuck at a lower stratum, the energy also revolves at lower frequencies to maintain proximity with the consciousness. It has to be understood that consciousness and energy pervade throughout the body. Depending upon it, each cell of our body has definite consciousness and energy and functions accordingly. It further leads to intelligence and independent memory of each sub-particle of life. Further, the deeper the aspect of consciousness, the higher the level of energy that pervades through it. Lastly, the deeper the consciousness penetrates life, the higher the dimension of life that the holder of body or self may experience. Thus devoid of higher consciousness or intellect, life in turn reverberates to its low ebb and vice versa.

7. Re-alignment on the path of truth

After introducing the friends to major vikaras and also about the ill effects that these vikaras may cause to a person, Ramesh further said that these vikaras make people so preoccupied and restless that they never let divine thoughts to pour in. Man's sole purpose remains to satisfy them, and seldom can the person be saved from its clutches. These vikaras indeed act like a kaliya Naag whose mention is there in Krishna Leela, who had five faces and who continuously spit venom and made all of them unconscious whoever goes near it. Likewise, many talents are wasted when people remain engrossed in these vikaras and thus forget their real selves, which are the actual source of all joy and happiness and which unites us with our universal nature or truth.

After listening to the narrative of Ramesh regarding the body and the five senses emanating from it, Sukhnandan became perplexed. Till then, Sukhnandan had known only about happiness, which is created by fulfilling the basic desires sprouting from one's bodily needs and mind. According to him, this body is the source of all joy, and we must perform such activities that enhance its joy and abstain from all such activities that do not provide joy to the body. So he got confused and questioned Ramesh as to whether there is a need to abstain from any impulse that is occurring naturally. He instead stressed doing hard work so that we may get the maximum of worldly endowments possible. This way we can enjoy our life, and if we have this precious human body, then we must embrace it by enjoying every flavour of life. This is indeed the best way to serve the Godly Plan. Whoever has seen the other world only knows that whatever is there, it is here and now. So he asked in amusement if there is any other happiness besides body and mind. He further enquired from Ramesh about one's true nature and how it is different from one's basic bodily nature.

To this, Ramesh replied that if you think yourself to be a body, then you can never enjoy eternal joy or bliss. How is it possible for such a person to remain permanently happy as this body is itself subject to the law of destruction, and thus happiness and sorrow are in detachable parts of this destructible body? Even if we relate our body to our limited mind, even then thoughts and emotions would continue to bother us and would decide our destiny and not the universal laws. Thus, body and mind are both subject to change and are limited by the time and space to which they actually belong. If we truly want to enjoy the permanent joy, then we have to identify ourselves beyond this body and mind. When all ignorance is shunted, then only we can encounter truth in its original form, which is devoid of ignorance and is based upon pure consciousness or knowledge of self. It is only when this truth is followed that we understand our eternal nature of permanence, self-illumination, and eternal bliss. This completeness of being cannot be experienced by merely living at the level of senses or mind.

Sukhnandan agreed that he had tried to live with all flavours of life, but still, it is true that he still lacks many things in life, and there is no completeness of being either. Despite being fully devoted to life, it did not remain always fair, and he has lost many precious things in life, which have filled him with deep agony and made him unfulfilled somewhere deep inside.

Interrupting in between Lokesh tried to add to Sukhnandan's earlier viewpoint and said that he also does not know whether we remain after the end of this body. He believed in the presence of God and that he believes that God has created this world for their enjoyment, and if they do not enjoy the things of amusements present in this world, then in a way we are betraying ourselves. He adds on to say that this life is very precious, and we must try to preserve it through any means possible. He strongly believed that all this world emanates from God and merges into it as soon as the person dies, so this body is the only existence that he believes to be, and that good and bad only belong to this world, so one must only strive to feed this body, physically, mentally, and morally, so that one can enjoy its existence, and one should try to legitimately fulfil all desires and cravings in this limited time frame that has been allotted to mankind.

Ramesh now exhorted that reality is not as we see it; it is indeed beyond our perception. It is not that we have an end or a beginning. The difference is only of appearance. It is only because of avidya (ignorance) that it appears so. We become what we perceive we are. However, in the absence of true knowledge, we always consider ourselves to be limited and dependent upon time and space. However, in actuality, we are beyond any of such dimensions. Time and space only affect us till we have not realised ourselves as souls. Indeed, a fully realised soul is beyond this dimension and remains unaffected by remaining connected to a universal cosmic force. One who realises its potential can never get devoured by the forces of ignorance and instead lives in consonance with nature. The reality is that we are part and parcel of the almighty, whose every essence is as complete as the divine itself and which cannot be devoured of its existence, potential, or understanding as well. When we have become truth, then we align with universal principle, and it never happens that universal principle becomes subjugated to any law. It is only when we deviate from our path that we become subjugated, and even in that case, if we have truly surrendered before the universal cosmic force, then sooner or later we get out of our ignorance that has caused havoc in our lives and be able to become part and parcel of supreme existence. Why do we have to hanker after happiness outside when we are the source of all eternal happiness and bliss? We are ourselves blissful when we are complete.

Many people fall prey to ignorance because they do not fully trust the supreme will, and in a hurry, they indulge in such wrong activities whose fruit they have to reap at later times. We must show full trust in the almighty. We should trust that whatever he chooses for us is in our best interest. We should not question his supreme will, as it only bestows upon us its infinite grace. We must remember that in early childhood, when we were not able to think and care for ourselves; even during that moment of life, God nourished us in the form of our parents and near and dear ones. Further, during our old age, we will not be able to think and take care of ourselves. Again, at that moment, God will be there to protect and nourish us, may be in some other form. Then why do we get afraid in between? Is it that our awareness of our body or our ego causes us to do that? Our mind and intellect, having been engrossed in the attachment of the body, forget about the universal principal, which is nourishing every creation that belongs to it. Our real nature is Sat chit Ananda, which we have forgotten by over-identifying with our body or its relations. **'Sat' tells us about our universal existence or immortality of the soul; 'chit' is our consciousness or knowledge about our existence; and 'Ananda' is the bliss, which is the true nature of our existence and the quality of our soul.**

a) Cover of Ignorance

This life is bound by karmas. To lead life in an effective way, we must know the pattern of life based upon righteousness. We should be conscious of the purpose of our life and in which direction it has to be led to make it successful. But seldom are we given true teachings of life. Our main motto remains to earn bread and butter so that we continue to survive in this body without ever bothering to know our real purpose of coming into being. We never experience completeness of being, which is our divine nature and from which sprouts eternal peace and bliss.

Essentially, this life is largely enveloped by ignorance. What we see and feel is only a minuscule part of reality. We recognise ourselves as a body that is only composed of five gross elements (ether, air, fire, water, and earth) and bodily sense organs, which are also in turn borne out from the subtler form of these five elements, or Tanmatras. All the knowledge that we acquire is how we perceive reality based on these senses. Thus, our whole knowledge remains confined to information received by our sense organs only. Further, the mind, being entrapped in this body, looks at these bodily senses to acquire the knowledge of self. Thus the self that would be worked out remains confined to our body and remains dependent upon it for its survival.

The mind, thus, misidentifies with the body and tries to find happiness only in satisfying the objects of its senses. As the mind remains preoccupied in sensual pleasure, it in turn gives rise to vikaras, which is the only outcome of over- or under-fixation of energy with objects of these senses.

Fundamentally, outer reality is transient and subject to change. However, we largely recognise the outer world and belong ourselves to things or people outside. We feel that these would give us eternal peace and satisfaction in life. But with every outer possession lies the fear of its losing. When the things or people we embrace depart from our lives for any reason, we feel immense pain out of bereavement, which far exceeds the joy that we once felt when we were united with them. **After facing a lot of setbacks, the mind starts looking for real knowledge, which may give him contentment and everlasting peace and happiness, and thus treads the path of truth**.

True knowledge dawns when we see ourselves as independent of this body and as infinite and thus not confined only to space and time, which are occupied by our physical body. Understanding this, we do not remain confined to the limits imposed by this mortal body and instead perform our work to uplift ourselves and also our fellow beings.

Five sheaths or layers envelop the soul, or Koshas (from gross to more subtle), viz., Annamaya Kosha, Prana Kosha, Mano Kosha, Gyan Kosha, and Ananda Kosha, i.e., the physical, vital, mental, intellectual, and blissful bodies. The larger the sheath, the greater the force of externality, i.e., when consciousness enters the physical body, we are material in our outlook or totally body conscious. When we go inward, then we encounter more subtle layers and thus become conscious of our true nature as a universal spirit.

There is a story to explain these phases of the development of inner consciousness as narrated in Bhrigu Valli of the Tattiriya Upanishad. Bhriguvalli is what Varuna taught to his son, Bhrigu. In this narrative, Bhrigu was curious to know the Brahman (Soul). With this intention in his mind, he approached his father Varuna and requested to introduce him to the Brahman. On this varuna disclosed that Brahman or

Brahm can be realised after delving within through tapa or penance. Taking advice from his Father, Bhrigu, he went for penance, and after spending a long time in introspection, he came to understand that the Anna (food) we take is Brahman, as all the world, even human beings, emanates from food, and this body is nothing but Anna itself. Thus he thought that Brahman was Annamaya, and with this definition of Brahman in his mind, he returned to his father for validation. However, his father again advised him to further perform more austerities and to delve within to realise the true essence of Brahman. Taking words from his father, Bhrigu again went for penance, and this time he correlated vital energy, or prana shakti, to Brahman, as it is only through prana that life comes into force, and we perform every activity through prana shakti, and also this body can move through prana, or vitality. Thus Bhrigu now considered Brahman as Pranamaya and went to his father with this inference. Varuna, after listening to his son, told him that though he has taken a right step towards Brahman, he is still far from a true understanding of Brahman. He again advised his son to continue tapa, as only with tapa Brahman can be realised. After taking command from his father, he again went for Tapa, and after a lot of self-reflection this time, he found that the manas, or mind, is the brahman, as all thoughts and all desires emanate in the manas, and that even our body moves after taking commands from the mind. Thus prana also follows this mind, and thus mind is supreme, and it is Brahman through which life can take its course. Thus he again returned to his father, and this time with the conception that Brahman is manomaya. Finding his son getting closer to reality, he again asked his son that he was treading the right path and advised him to continue with the penance to realise the actual state of Brahman. So after taking the word from his father, he again undertook a lot of austerities, and this time he came across Buddhi and found that it is subtler than the manas as it uses the tools of reasoning, logic, and rationality and also guides manas about right and wrong based upon situations. So in a way, it gives direction to the manas and enlightens the manas to take a wise course. Thus he now came up with the new conclusion that Brahman is indeed Vijnanmaya and went to his father to confirm his affirmations. But this time also Varuna advised him again to delve within through penance to realise the Brahman. Adhering to the directions of his father, without losing his temperament, and like a true disciple, he again performed austerities, and this time he came closer to his being and realised that one's being, which is all blissful and free from mundane activities of life, is brahman, as it is not dependent upon body vitality, manas, and buddhi for receiving the happiness and is self-luminous and the source of all joy and bliss. He thus declared that Brahman is anandmaya, or all blissful, and with this assertion came back to his father. On listening to this definition of Brahman, Varuna felt so happy and proud of his son and told his son that now you have a glimpse of the actual state of Brahman.

The true self lies beyond anandamaya kosha, as Brahman is to be experienced and not known. Brahman is indeed the knower of all and yet cannot be known. So every time Bhrigu understood one kosha, his father Varuna told him to meditate more and understand the reasons why that kosha should not be considered the ultimate. It is only after Bhrigu understood that the quality of Brahman is anandamaya; did Varuna tell Bhrigu that his quest for the ultimate is over.

In the innermost core lies the Atma, which largely remains a witness entity unless a person delves within and removes all the layers of ignorance and illusion. We recognise more with our body and individual mind, and thus all our lives we consider ourselves to be a limited phenomenon. Even the knowledge that rests in our intellect is also based upon our sense organs and confined to this body only and is seldom based upon universal laws. In the same way, our happiness is also dependent upon fulfilling our desires emanating from bodily needs. Thus, the Upanishads very well explain our mundane existence and specifically target our dependence upon this body for all our happiness, consciousness, and existence. However, after realising its vast potential as Braham, or soul, the self bestows with existence beyond bodily limits, knowledge of the vast cosmos, and eternal bliss that is not dependent upon limits imposed by time, space, or name and forms. These states of consciousness have been variously mentioned as asti, bhati, and priya, corresponding to Sat chit Anand. However, this state of being requires one to work further to realise one's soul as part and parcel of the almighty, the state which is beyond the state of Brahm and known as Par Brahm, where a soul, after merging with the supreme soul itself, becomes supreme (Parmatma).

In this regard, in order to have experience of Brahman, the Mandukya Upanishad talks about four states of consciousness, viz., jagrut, svapna, sushupti, and turiya:

1. In the Jagrut state, we misidentify Brahm as the external reality. We experience the outside world through nineteen tools of consciousness, which are 5 jnana indriyas (senses of knowledge), 5 karma indriyas (organs of action), 5 pranas, and four operations of the psyche, viz., Manas, Buddhi, Ahamkara, and Chitta. Consciousness grasps objects from outside through these nineteen mouths—nineteen aspects. In this state, Brahm is mainly misidentified with the physical body.

2. In the state of Swapna, the direct link with outer reality is broken. However, Prana, Manas, and Buddhi are activated in the dream state. In this state, Brahm is misidentified by Pranamaya kosha, Manomaya kosha, and Vijananamaya kosha.

3. In deep sleep or the state of sushupti, only the causal sheath is active, i.e., Anandamaya kosha.

4. Turiya is the 4th state where there is no misidentification with any of the koshas. Thus there is pure experience that is devoid of any ignorance. This is the state of eternal bliss and corresponds to Parbrahm. Here the states of Alakh, Agam, and Agochar are experienced, which are the qualities of a soul and are also unachievable, indescribable, and unreachable through the mind. This state is experienced only when the mind surrenders all its

actions, conceptions, thoughts, emotions, and desires or will to the supreme. This is the highest state of being where a person does not recognise even with one's achievements, one's knowledge, or devotion. Here the person eradicates all its identity, merges in the divine reality, and experiences one's cosmic presence in the form of eternal bliss.

Again, the Taitreya Upanishad deals with this subject. The five koshas have been classified into three groups: the physical, the subtle, and the causal, corresponding to three worlds. In the physical plane lies the Annamaya kosha. In the astral sphere lie Pranamaya Kosha, Manomaya Kosha, and Vijananamaya Kosha. Whereas, in the causal sphere lies only Anandamaya kosha.

In a similar fashion, Bharthari Rishi has also talked about 4 types of sound energies engulfing all life and creation. The first sound is vaikhari. Everything that we say or every mantra that we enchant physically belongs to this sound. It corresponds to the state of Jagrut, or conscious mind. Next comes the sound of Madhyama, which corresponds to the mental state of being. Here the sound exists only on the thinking level and is yet not expressed. All the thoughts, plans, and emotions that we made in our minds but yet not expressed come under the category of Madhyama speech or sound. It corresponds to the state of the subconscious, or also Swapna. The next comes the sound of pashayanti, which exists only as an idea and is

unmanifasted. **This corresponds to the state of Sushupti (the dreamless sleep when the unconscious mind takes over). The last sound is para, which corresponds to the state of Turiya, which is also known as ParBrahma or Shabda Brahm. Thus, when we are ultimately able to listen to this subtle sound, or Shabda Brahma, reverberating at the Brahmrandhra, then we can merge into supreme reality or merge with ParBrahm.**

Further, these sounds exist at a very subtle level and can be experienced through raising the consciousness to its highest level. The most subtle of all sounds is para, or transcendental, followed by pashyanti (which can be seen, observed, and visualised), then madhyama (intermediate), and ultimately vaikhari (articulate sound). In the field of spirituality, these four sounds also take precedence. First of all, when we enchant a sacred mantra orally, then it takes the form of vaikhari. After the mantras are mastered, these mantras are recited mentally without making use of bodily instruments. At this stage, it corresponds to Madhyama. When this mental recitation also vanishes, here the mantra recites on their own, and only their awareness is left here. This state marks the Pashyanti. Lastly, when all creation merges with their source, then what remains is all bliss. This is the state of Para and is the eternal blissful state of Par Brahm.

8. Reunion with Nature

Ramesh tried to explain to his friends about the inward journey from the physical plane towards subtle aspects of life and ultimately towards the soul. As the person moves inwards and gains consciousness, he comes closer to ultimate reality and finally merges with its source as he gains a complete understanding of himself. Thus the spiritual journey of a person is from ignorance to knowledge, where the knowledge also encompasses full awareness of self together with realisation of innate potential.

After listening to the narrative of Ramesh, both Lokesh and Sukhnandan became perplexed and yet a little impressed. Further, they asked Ramesh where from he has learnt these mysteries of life, which you claim to be based upon truth. To this, Ramesh replied that he has learnt the basis of truth or spirituality from his mentor, who has shared with him the deepest secrets of spirituality. Not only this, but my mentor also taught me the right direction of life along with the right approach to things. My mentor introduced me to Paramatma not only in terms of faith but also in terms of a universal principle based upon Shabd Brahm. To reach this transcendental state of being, my mentor initiated me with a mantra of Aum enchanting. The whole creation has come into being through this transcendental sound. Thus, reality can be easily understood when we board the vehicle of Aum, which takes us directly to the seed of creation by following the royal road of the Sushmana canal, which flows in the middle of the backbone. This is the evolutionary journey of the mind from being an individual mind that is entrenched with Panch vikaras to becoming a universal mind that flows in consonance with universal laws and is independent of all samskaras and vikaras. Thus this journey is from being individual to becoming universal, where one sheds his ego and tunes one's life in terms of universal laws and becomes the soul.

a) Individuality has to give its way to become universal.

As individuals, we can never cross the barrier imposed by nature. But as a part of the whole, we can direct nature the way we want it to, or we can become nature itself. When we surrender to a universal source, then it automatically absolves every one of our problems. We must impose trust on God and his greater will. If he has nurtured and taken care of us to date, then he will continue to do so. Even if some harm is inflicted upon us, it is again for our betterment and to make us a better person. Don't ever question the will of God. It is for the best of mankind.

My mentor used to say that when we get to know that all the positivity reflects godliness, then we have attained the state of super consciousness. However, when we finally make out that even negativity is the essence of God and works only on God's plan, then we have attained a supreme consciousness state. Indeed, negativity teaches us the best. lessons of life, which positivity cannot do. It teaches us the worth of our faith in the Supreme Lord. It checks our faith. If our belief is limited to our ego, then we can never cross the barrier imposed by negativity. However, if it is rooted in the Almighty and based upon self-surrender and truth, then it gives us a new direction of life. Thus only those who have complete faith in God pass this last exam of nature or primordial divine power. Those who are proud only of their capabilities and skills get swayed by the negative forces of nature, whose role it is to end individuality or ego in all its forms and instead give way to universal principles based upon truth. The faith that we put in the supreme lord never goes without bearing fruit, and this faith taking the form of inner divine light enlightens the way even in utter darkness.

However, we must be cautious and slow in performing spiritual austerities. If we deserve and have requisite characteristics, we would even get to the universal consciousness of being in a fraction of a second. Again, if we lack the requisite characteristics, then even a thousand years would not suffice. So we should be settled in our minds and not overexcited. Moreover, we must always take refuge in the Almighty and always surrender our body, mind, spirit, and all that we have before the Supreme. Only then can we receive the grace of the almighty, which then enlightens our way and also wards off or silences all the evil spirits or whomever tries to inflict harm on us.

My mentor once told us to never be in a hurry in the field. of spirituality, as it could pose harm to us. He further asserted that even if you can't see God, God definitely sees you. So what is the hurry to reach to God?

Just try to gain consciousness with each passing day, and once you are worthy of it, Mother Nature will itself disclose the divine plan before you. Till then, if you have surrendered before God or truth, then the same would protect you from all the unforeseen miseries of life. Further, the nature of self is silence, and speed only enthrals the mind and not the spirit. Those who want to claim spiritual heights through stubbornness end up attracting a lot of miseries and discomforts of life.

Pertinent to mention here that we keep negativity alongside us in the form of our weaknesses. This most often catches our mind and keeps us vibrating at lower frequencies, which is an ideal place for evil forces to prosper. With time, this negativity keeps strengthening and takes the form of evil. When we channel our energies for higher frequencies, then the problems of our lives automatically subside.

One more thing has been noticed: when energy present in our bodies compromises (especially due to the seeds of inactivity), then we get stuck into lower energy levels where we face a lot of troubles that are otherwise unwarranted to us. Thus we must always try to raise our energy vis-à-vis. our consciousness so that we can overcome unwanted miseries of life that have been caused by a lack of energy and consciousness. The energies at the lower level of consciousness flow abruptly and cause inertia, or tamas. The energy at its optimum level makes us satvik, and when intermediary, then rajsik.

9. The Self

The self is the source of all attraction. The body loses all its attraction as soon as this self leaves the body. The mind is the firstborn son of self. However, due to over-attachment to the mind, the self has turned into a witness entity despite being the reason for the existence of life and, in turn, the mind. The self has become subservient to the mind, which in turn is hankering after to satisfy the bodily desires borne out of various instincts and passions. For this self to realise its actual position as soul, there is a need to first emancipate the mind to settle at its exalted state at the trikuti centre or centre of the forehead, where it acts according to the universal laws of nature.

It doesn't mean that we start ignoring our bodily needs. However, the problem arises when we become so attached to the body that we forget our real identity as souls and become only the toy of nature and dance on the whims and fancies dictated by the mind. Till our mind remains much engrossed with the body, then it remains confined to the forewall of one's ego and thus only satisfies the bodily needs through any means. In this state, the mind can never spare time for self-realisation as it always remains overly dependent upon various forces of nature to fulfil its unending desires. Further, due to a lack of self-realisation, the person may commit so many mistakes that it would not remain easy to realise one's being.

Again, till the mind is not free from the bondage of vikaras associated with bodily senses, the mind can never fully settle at the Trikuti centre, and the self also has to struggle to realise the actual state till then. This vicious cycle never seizes till the strong thirst for one's self sprouts from within. **This happens only when the mind finds that it cannot find real joy anywhere outside, as every outside state is momentary and carries with it agony and fear of losing.**

The self is the source of all attraction in our body. But due to our limited awareness, which is confined only to our bodies, our self has to depend upon the mind to realise its actual state since there are innumerable impressions on our mind that never let us fully concentrate upon our real nature. Thus the self has become mere a witness entity and has become a tool of the mind and intellect, which in turn is governed by various instincts and sensual passions. Till the mind is not free from these junk thoughts, it does not give way for the self to realise its actual position.

Now talking about the Vaishvanara self, or the universal being, the Upanishad talks about such a state of consciousness where we contemplate the whole universe as our body. This is the later stage of the development of consciousness, where we see ourselves as a universal whole. Where eyes have been contemplated as sun, head as heaven, Prana as air, body as Akasha, lower belly as water, and feet as earth.

There is a story mentioned in the Brihadaranyaka Upanishad in which there lived five great sages who had done a lot of austerities, but they were not still sure about Brahman. So they decided to go to Uddaalaka as they knew that Uddalaka had done great studies on Brahman and that he could cast away their queries related to the final take on the conceptualisation of Brahman. When Uddalaka saw these five great sages coming towards his hut, he instantly understood that they must be coming to clear their doubts related to Brahman. Uddalaka had done a lot of studies on Brahman through performing austerities for several years, but he was still unclear on some points, and he knew that since the sages were well versed or masters in the spiritual field, they could make him confused somewhere. So as these saints reached near to Uddalaka and told them their reason for coming to him, Uddalaka at once told them that although he knew many things about Brahman, he still had certain doubts related to the actual position of Brahman. He further suggested that they must go to their king Ashvapati, as the king, besides serving his countrymen, also has great spiritual knowledge related to Brahman, and he can certainly make us clear on Brahman. So they all proceeded to the court of King Ashvapati and told the king that they had come for the knowledge of Vaishvanara Atman.

Ashvapti agreed to teach them, and on the next day, the rishis approached the king as pupils. Ashvapati addressed each of these sages separately to find out about their sadhana and then explained to each of them about Vaishvanara Atman in terms of their object of meditation. King Ashvapati told one of the disciples that the self that he meditates upon as heaven is the head of the Vaisvanara self. To the second disciple who meditates upon the sun as the Self, he says that the Self meditated upon by him is the universal form and is the eye of the Vaisvanara Self. To the third disciple who meditates upon the air as self, he says that the self meditated upon is the breath or the Prana of the Vaisvanara self. To the fourth disciple who meditates upon Akasha as the Self, he confirms that the Self meditated upon is the body of the Vaisvanara Self. The fifth disciple who meditates upon water as the Self explained that his object of meditation is the lower belly of the Vasvanara Self. To the sixth disciple, uddalaka, who meditates upon earth as the self, he explained that the object of his self-meditation is the feet of the vaisvanara self.

Finally, pointing to the limitations of the knowledge of these Rishis, he said to them that it is not by meditating on parts that one can know all. The truth is known when all is seen. Therefore, realising the whole consists of all parts one has the experience of Vaishvanara Atman.

Do not impose thoughts or pressure the mind to concentrate on specific positions of the body; that way we may never come out of the fascinations of the mind, and our mind would never come to a standstill.

We may increase the capacity of our mind through

performing kriya yoga techniques (especially enchanting of Aum), and once we realise our innate mental capacity, we should always pave the way for our innate nature to take its own course. Here we only observe the phenomenon taking place within our body and try to listen to inner divine sound.

Enchanting of aum or sacred mantras opens our energy centres, and thus we can receive divine grace in the form of nectar flowing in the cosmos. Thus, to realise our full potential, we must first purify and open all our energy centres through enchanting sacred mantras or following certain kriya yoga techniques, and then observe our true nature as it is. Pertinent to mention here that our true nature is truth when we are flowing the same inward and outward. When we are one with mind, speech, and action, then only we can get acquainted with our true selves and realise our full potential. Thus we must develop ourselves in such a way that we understand and follow the universal laws (truth) in any given situation so that our energy does not get stuck anywhere and flows proportionately within ourselves.

a) Knowledge as Brahman

It is said that one who knows Brahman becomes Brahman. A person can realise Brahman only when one is free from all illusions and delusions. It is when one, after crossing all sheaths of ignorance, immerses into one's true being.

The Brahman is the conscious state of nothingness or an un-sprouted realised state, in which the cosmic energy or sound stream flows automatically and makes it blissful and, through their amalgamation, becomes enlightened. From this blissful state, the whole universe had its origin and was finally submerged into it.

In between, life gains its momentum through the interactional forces of consciousness and intelligence. Through this nothingness, life survives and maintains its value in the form of perfect order, where any minute deviation disturbs the whole life cycle and results in devastation and chaos. Thus, while we should be conscious of our divine aspect, it is also prudent to be able to differentiate between all aspects of life and understand the balance that needs to be struck between them. Only then does life survive and order remains intact, which gives further way for life to flourish. Thus intelligence and consciousness work in unison to systematically maintain this order and form a discipline that further survives life.

Once, Raja Janak invited Vedic scholars from far-off countries concerning certain rituals and announced that he would give enormous wealth and riches to the one who could prove himself/herself to be the best Vedic scholar among all. Where none of the scholars could rise and claim to be the best, Maharishi Yajnavalakya stood up and asked one of his disciples to collect all the rewards and take them home. He further pronounced that he bows before the person who claims to be supreme Bhram Gyani or best Vedic scholar, but he is taking the rewards as they are much needed in his ashram. With this, a debate gets started between various scholars and Maharishi Yajnavalkya. Many great scholars, including Ashwala and Uddalaka, put a lot of questions to the Yajnavalakya, which were correctly answered by him and up to the satisfaction of all the scholars. There was also present one woman scholar named Vachanku Gargi, who also asked a lot of questions, which were all answered by Yajnavalkya Ji. At last, Gargi said that she would ask the sage two more questions, and if he would answer them, none of the scholars present there would ever be able to beat him.

Gargi asked, "O Sage, what pervaded the whole cosmos, which also encompasses the past, present, and future?" Yajnavalkya replied, "The unmanifested ether."

"Gargi bowed before him and praised for the satisfactory reply."

"Gargi again asked."

"What pervades the unmanifested ether?"

The sage replied, "IT is pervaded by the immutable Brahman. It is neither gross nor subtle, neither short nor long, neither air nor ether; it is devoid of all attributes yet. all find their basis in it. The different worlds, the sun and the moon, do not transgress its mighty rule and operate at its will. Whoever departs from this world without Knowing or experiencing this immutable state remains enmeshed in illusion and has to move in the vicious cycle of births and deaths. It is the knower who knows through all intellects. Brahman, which is the self within all and is beyond all relative attributes like hunger, etc., is the ultimate goal, the highest truth. By this, Brahman is the unmanifested ether pervaded."

Thereupon Gargi said, "Revered Brahmins, listen to my words. I have already said that if he can answer my questions, none of you can beat him. You can never hope to defeat him. In comprehending Brahman, he has no peer."

It has to be understood that when all the sheaths of illusions are burned in the fire of knowledge, then what remains behind is the immutable Brahman. Brahman is beyond time and space and instead controls it. Not a thought can take flight in the mind of a person without its permission. It pervades through the cosmos and is the supreme controller of all beings and non-beings. It is the ultimate reality before which every other reality finds its roots. It is an immutable and immortal state of being and survives in the face of all destructions and emancipations.

Two primal elements and their evolution

There is a reason behind everything, and everything that exists has a definite cause. If we take Brahman as a state of infinite consciousness, then around its extremity life flourishes in the form of possibilities and on the basis of level of awareness. Thus, the extremity that is created momentarily through conceiving this immutable state also causes its counterpart in the form of primordial divine potency to come into being.

This primordial divine potency, or divine energy, in proximity with divine consciousness expresses itself in the form of three principles. Where there is life, this divine power is called Brahma; where there is love and nourishment, the same divine energy is called Vishnu; and where there is knowledge and distinction between right and wrong, the same is called Shiva.

In Samkhya there is mention of two opposite forces or elements, viz., Purusha and Prakriti. The essence of Purusha is light or consciousness, and the essence of Prakriti is potency or activity. Further, all seeds of creation are embedded in Prakriti, which reflects itself in the form of three gunas or qualities, viz., Satva, Rajas, and Tamas, which are inherent in Prakriti. However, these gunas or qualities are present in the prakriti in a balanced state, which is called trigunatmika.

When the light or consciousness of Purusha falls on Prakriti, its constituents, viz., Gunas, get disturbed, which then leads to the creation of the whole universe, or samsara. Fundamentally, when the light of Purusha comes into contact with Prakriti, a new element called Mahat is created. This is the first evolution of Mula Prakriti or Pradhan Prakriti (Prakriti is called Pradhan or Mool as all the creation has roots in it). In Mahat tatva, there is a predominance of Satva Guna, which is also called cosmic intelligence.   This state is marked by the presence of self-awareness This Satva Guna further leads to the creation of Rajo Guna, which is expressed in the form of activity. Through intermingling of Satva and Rajas, the third guna, viz., Tamas, comes to view whose quality is inactivity or neutrality.

Further, from Rajo Guna 5 Karam Indriyas, from Sato Guna 5 Gyan Indriyas, and from Tamo Guna 5 Tanmatras (subtle aspects of Panch Mahabhutas) are created. Again, collectively, Sato guna gives rise to Antahkaran, viz., Manas (thoughts and anti-thoughts), Buddhi (determination), Ahamkar (individuality), and Chitta (including memories or past impressions). Whereas Rajo Guna collectively gives rise to 5 pranas, viz., Prana, Apana, Samana, Udana, and Vyana. Tamo guna gives rise to 5 Maha Bhutas (whose subtle aspects are Tanmatras), viz., ether, air, fire, water, and earth. It is pertinent to mention here that this whole gross universe is the result of these Panch Mahabhutas.

Furthermore, Mahat Tattva leads to the creation of the ego, which further leads to the creation of the individual mind. Once the ego, or individual I, is formed, the cosmic intelligence, or mahat, becomes buddhi and turns into individualised awareness based upon individual intelligence.

Again, this ego or individuality gets hold of all the Gunas, which in turn becomes the cause of all miseries, viz., Adhyatamik miseries, which are inflicted due to ailment of body and mind; Adhidaivik miseries are due to natural disturbances, viz., earthquakes, tsunamis, floods, etc.; and adhibhautik miseries that are caused by other living entities.

Distribution of 25 elements as per Samkhya Darshan

Avikriti (non-transformational): Mula Prakriti or Pradhan is not the effect of another Tatva, so it is called Avikriti. So it is the cause itself.

Avikriti-Vikriti: Mahat,   Ahamkara,   and   5 Tanmatras—they are the cause of other lower tatvas and themselves are also effects of some cause. From Mahat Ahamkar is created, which in turn is the cause of mind. Similarly, from 5 Tanmatras, 5 Mahabhutas are created.

Vikriti: 5 Gyan Indriyas, 5 karma Indriyas, mind, and 5 Mahabhutas.

Thus, the 24 above Tatvas elements, together with Purusha, constitute the 25 elements of nature.

So in this way, one pattern supports the other, and thus life is interwoven, which sustains itself till the impact of perceived consciousness remains embedded in the psyche or till an undiluted state of consciousness is not attained. When such an undiluted state is achieved, then the one is called brahm gyani. However, the knowledge of Brahm or Brahm Gyan also encapsulates Tatva Gyan, as complete knowledge of self cannot be attained without full understanding of all the tatvas or evolutes of Prakriti or constituents of primordial divine power. However, such knowledge is always attained by delving inside and thereby understanding the core concept of each such aspect, not superficially through reading of scriptures or from hearsay. Till mind (here it means Ahamkar, Buddha, Chitta, and Man) is engrossed or under the influence of any of the tatva, it cannot fully surrender its operations before universal cause, primal cause, or Param Atma. This causes attachment to the different aspects of nature and an inability to concentrate on the true self, viz., truth. Thus our sole purpose is to understand the true essence of self and immerse in it while not limiting oneself to the Maya or worldly illusion. Maya, or nature, is the mirror that reflects the essence of the soul or light. Thus, Maya in itself is neither true nor untrue; however, it is the pure potency to realise the truth.

Antahkaran or Chitta (which also includes Man, Buddhi, Ahamkar, and Chitta)

Chitta (pure intelligence, or Mahat) is the storehouse of cosmic intelligence where one connects with the cosmos and has vast knowledge of different laws of the universe. However, due to chitta vrittis (mental fluctuations), a person is not able to attain this cosmic state. According to Patanjali, there are five types of vrittis that restrict a person from realising themselves:

1. **Pramana (correct knowledge)** Pramana, or correct knowledge, is attained in three ways:
a) Pratyaksha Pramana (attained through senses),
b) Anumana Pramaan (inference),
c) Agama Pramana (vedic knowledge or from the words of a guru)

Here the knowledge is not the outcome of pure experience but indirect and thus lacks insight.

2. **Viparaya (misconception under the influence of avidya or ignorance)** To become a seer, we should have understanding of jeeva, ishwara, and prakriti. The mind cannot be directed appropriately until the right understanding is attained.
3. **Vikalpa (conceptualisation, imagination)** Mind

4. cannot be settled till it does not surrender before self.
5. **Nidra (dream state or deep sleep)** In this state, we are not aware of the self. Due to a lack of knowledge, we don't witness a state of eternal bliss.
6. **Smriti (memory)** It dilutes our mind and does not let us experience a state of pure consciousness.

Further, these vrittis can either be painful (klishta causes klesha) or nonpainful (aklishta).

Klesha, or suffering, happens due to the following five reasons:

1. Avidya or Ignorance
2. Asmita means ego, considering Atma and Buddhi (Prakriti) as one
3. Raga means pleasure accompanying attachment. Dvesha means pain accompanying aversion.

4.Abhinivesha means fear of death (due to overidentification with limited existence or the gross physical body).

These virtues thus always affect one's ability to find the truth. Thus, they need to be neutralised through yogic techniques before attaining a pure state of intellect, or cosmic intelligence.

Further, under the influence of 3 Gunas, the chitta, or cognition, of a person rests on five seats known as chitta bhumis. Under the influence of Rajo Guna, the Chitta works on the principle of activity. This state is called kshipta, and the consciousness of a person resembles a monkey. Under the influence of Tamas Guna, the Chitta becomes passive or dormant. This is the phase of inactivity and is called Moodha. Here the state of consciousness resembles a donkey. When the Chitta oscillates between the activity phase and the inactivity phase, it is called vikshipta and comes immediately before the emergence of satwik guna. Here the chitta behaves like a butterfly. Under the influence of satwik guna, the Chitta becomes soothing and calm. This is the ekagra state of mind. The last state of chitta is beyond the influence of three gunas and is called Nirodha, or cessation of all vrittis.

b) Activity is the life

Life is not going to show us any miracles. We have to aspire and claim the rewards for our deeds. Knowledge alone would not take us anywhere, as it would only show us the right way. We can't intermingle different phenomena. Not only intentions and knowledge, but right action is also required. We have to do and get the things done. If we are doing the right things, then we would get results instantly; otherwise, hundred years of waiting would also not suffice. We have to become the masters of our destiny. Don't shy away from putting in maximum efforts to open the doors of fortune. Those who wait for conducive time to come will never be able to achieve what they truly deserve. Thus, make the time conducive through efforts and go and get the course of destiny to flow in your favour. When the life reverberates at the maximum frequency, only then does it show us its true colours of Sat Chit Anand, which may sometimes be correlated with desire knowledge and action.

We cannot remain even a second without doing certain work. This world has come into existence only after gaining momentum. So every creature living or nonliving is unconsciously participating in this phenomenon and harnessing energy. Every atom of the universe is continuously reverberating and ensuring its existence.

Activity is of various types. In the base of evolution, one put efforts only for material existence. As the person climbs the ladder, it gains consciousness, and now it also puts efforts into gaining vitality through channelling. Prana, viz., prana, apana, udana, samman, and vyana. He also tunes his mind or thoughts and puts them under conscious control. He then channels the intellect and attunes it with universal laws. So we see that by gaining more knowledge about oneself, a person can give the right direction to the activity. But in any scenario, activity is a must. If we do not perform actions under our conscious control, then the forces of inactivity automatically start to function and start disturbing all equilibrium of life and creating entropy and chaos in our lives. So it is our prime duty to uplift ourselves after gaining knowledge and channelling our energy in the right direction.

One thing to remember always is that we should not bother to control the outcome of our efforts. Rather, we should only try to give our best in any particular situation by putting in the right efforts and then leaving the burden of outcome on nature. It is the law of nature that whatever seed we give to nature embraces the seed and provides nourishment, and as it starts blossoming, it returns the same to us with dividends. It is indeed the work of nature to create, nourish, and then dissolute everything that belongs to nature. We only trigger nature to perform such actions for us, whether in the mental realm or at the level of the gross physical world. So always remember that our efforts never go wasted, and we always come up with the best results in due course of time and as a reward from nature. That's why nature is also called the consort of consciousness.

Thus, it also becomes necessary that we put efforts in the right direction, as if we take the wrong course, then its result would be equally devastating when it bears fruit. So with the passing of every single day, we must ensure that our level of consciousness is raised through proper reflection of ourselves so that we may not indulge in wrong karmas unknowingly. The Upanishad says that we must do penance to understand ourselves and to raise our consciousness. Penance here means the transformation of our energy from low level to high and then to higher and ultimately to highest. It is only possible. when our mind is not deviated or under the influence of any vikara, which means our concentration should be undiluted. Activity thus encapsulates our vital body, mind, intellect, self, higher self, and so on, and not merely our physical or material body.

A vast potential lies dormant within us, and we can realise it at any time by making constant and rightful efforts. It is pertinent to mention here that it is up to us to choose which life we call for ourselves. We can live a wayward and meaningless life where we always move hither and thither and flow with the direction of the wind or circumstances. On the contrary, we can also live a meaningful and great life by building ourselves. Always remember that nature only provides us with what we deserve. The respect we can only earn when we raise our consciousness through daily efforts, which makes us masters of our destiny and not enslaved by circumstances and time. In the lower stratum of consciousness, the control of nature is predominant, as it is devoid of true knowledge and only instincts and desires control us, which only belong to our base nature. As we raise our consciousness, we also start to channelise the different aspects of nature, viz., Sat, Raj, and Tam, and after gaining full or pure consciousness, we become the masters of our nature or the circumstances around us. We can thus take our life in any direction in relation to whatever we want because when we understand the various laws of nature and implement them in our day-to-day lives, then nature becomes conducive to us and functions as per our will.

Again, the level of consciousness that we have realised remains with us irrespective of bodily limits imposed by time, space, distance, and death. However, activity is a must to realise our full potential. Knowledge remains futile if it is not followed by its proper implementation. Thus action, or kriya, is a must for realising the state of eternal bliss, which cannot be bestowed upon us as a gift but as the outcome of our deeds.

Again, we may also ponder whether we are inherently designed to achieve excellence in any field or that our lives are primarily decided by luck. In this context, we have to understand that our fate always works relatively rather than absolutely. Our fate itself is decided by our preparation to deal with certain life situations. It is the fact that we are all designed in certain unique ways based upon the arrangement of our genes, which may give us an edge over certain aspects of life. But even if we have proclivity to excel in certain fields, we may or may not realise those aspects of life based upon our efforts and priorities that we give to them. Nevertheless, when we put our efforts in the right direction, we can easily change the course of our fate or destiny. Thus, we must always put in the right efforts in life in order to become masters of our destinies. Again, when we are on the righteous path, then the grace of Almighty always comes by and guides our way.

Sometimes, even when we get many comforts of life, we may get distracted from our goals as we get used to it with the passage of time and forget about our real duties and goals. We all must know about Giskinda Naresh Sugreev, who was a devout devotee of Ram. But after Bali got killed by Ram, Sugreev became so engrossed in enjoying his riches and luxuries of life that he momentarily forgot his commitment that he had made before Raja Ram to trace Mata Sita and get them back after fighting the demon king Ravan.

Thus, luxuries or attainments also sometimes block our way if we do not know how to handle them carefully. Thus, one must always remain cautious about their prime goals, and any blessing on the way should be treated as a cornerstone in uniting with the cause and not turned into an impediment to fully realising one's self.

To reunite with our supreme state or nature is a long process as it is followed by the highest consciousness and intelligence, which can be bestowed only after following the righteous path and is also subject to the development of the body, mind, and soul. However, before treading the spiritual path, the mind must have a glimpse of reality that can be bestowed when, after delving in, the mind or consciousness touches all the spiritual centres, starting from Muladhar up to Trikuti (lying in the forehead) and via the Sushmana Canal, under the supervision of a realised saint. The easiest way to understand one's real position vis-à-vis the cosmos is through regular enchanting of sacred Aum Mantra for five to ten minutes in the morning and evening. Through Aum's regular enchanting, the mind may traverse the secret path of sushmana, starting from the Muladhara chakra lying at the coccyx centre or tail of the backbone and up to Trikuti, and thereafter till the fontanelle or top of the head through Brahmrandra. While traversing its upward journey, the mind may be introduced to various spiritual centres and also have a glimpse of the constitution and workings of these centres. After reaching to the top and after getting known the truth, the mind again starts the reverse course where It attains mastery over all the different aspects, which is sin qua not for making a permanent settlement of consciousness and one's immersion into Supreme reality. All these aspects are universal laws where one gives way to another and helps in the survival of nature and, in turn, life.

Everything that has life has prana. All spiritual experiences that we undergo become possible only after lifting this prana. There are many techniques in kriya yoga for uplifting the prana to its subtle level. It is pertinent to mention here that prana should be able to flow freely in the sushmana nadi, which flows in our backbone. Only when prana flows freely in this canal do we have experience of spirituality. According to the

Vedas, there are three knots, or Granthis, that obstruct prana from entering into sushmana nadi and rising. The Brahma Granti restricts the prana between Muladhar and Swadhistan. This knot restricts Mana to entering into muladhar and then to swadhistha. Once the prana crosses the Brahma Granthi, the next comes Vishnu Granthi. Here the consciousness remains struck between the manipura chakra and the anahat chakra. The last knot belongs to Rudra and is called Rudra Granthi. This knot restricts the prana to enter into Guru chakra and sahasrara chakra and restricts the prana between Anahat chakra and Ajna chakra. The main purpose of yogic techniques is to purify the energy channels so that Pranas flow freely through out the body and lead to realisation of self.

Various kriya yoga techniques to uplift Prana

Aum Enchanting: The enchanting of aum is the royal vehicle to connect the mind with the self. It is done in three forms. Initially, there is physical enchanting of aum. In this, the person crosses all spiritual centres and lastly crosses the physical plane when all chakras are activated in the physical plane. After that, a person enters the mental sphere, where the enchanting is done in the form of the flow of pranas in the sushmana nadi and there by channelling their flow to have deeper experiences of self. The last enchanting is the listening of divine sound inside our body. It has to be understood that all the spiritual centres vibrate at their own optimum frequency. However, owing to our marginal energy level, we cannot concentrate on inner divine sound. There are many sounds that reverberate inside our bodies, but here the talk is specifically about the sound associated with Shabda Brahma that reverberates in sahasrar, or head centre, which partakes when the mind seizes all its operations—either temporarily or for an extended period. of time—in which the person is specifically in a state of Samadhi. Thus, we should prepare our body and mind for such a state where we can listen to our inner divine sound and channelise our lives to dwell in that state. The same sound, when it becomes more vibrant and profound, explodes into inner divine light. Apt to mention here that during each state we must surrender before the universal cosmic energy and receive the divine grace in the form of universal nectar or cosmic energy, which floats every nook and cranny of the universe and starts flowing within us as soon as we attract it through self-surrender.

So Hum or Hamsa technique: This mantra is related to the advanced state and comes naturally to the person as soon as a person crosses the physical dimension of enchanting of aum. This is helpful for reaching the higher states, or, in that matter, the highest state of consciousness, and comes naturally when it is of use to the person. It is of help to a person to unite with one's self, which is also regarded as Hamsa or a swan.

Enchanting the mantra on hearsay without first being deserving can have its adverse effects as well.

Khechri mudra: This is one of many mudras that help a person to unite with certain spheres of consciousness. It is mostly associated with the vishuddhi chakra and helps a person to have a vast understanding of reality. In this mudra, the tongue is twisted upwards and touches the hard palate or beyond it. However, it should not be done forcefully and comes naturally to the sadhak when the chakra associated with it is trigred.

Shambhavi Mudra: In this mudra, the eyes are twisted upwards and focused to concentrate either between eyebrows (Ajna Chakra) or the centre of the forehead (guru chakra). This helps to raise the consciousness of a person, but such actions should be performed under the direct guidance of a spiritual mentor, as they may have adverse effects as well if the body is not prepared for them.

Mahabandha: In Mahabandha, three types of Bandha are operated, viz., Mool Bandha, Uddayin Bandha, and Jallandar Bandha. Through these bandhas, the energy starts flowing in the Mooladhara chakra, the Manipura chakra, and the Vishuddhi chakra, respectively. Paschimottanasana is the best kriya where these three bandhas can be easily operated.

Rechak, kumbhak, and Purak Pranayam: It is the method of purification of pranas in ida and pingala where the pranas are floated in both canals through both nostrils. When the breathed air, or prana, is inhaled, it is called Poorak. After taking the pranas upwards or inwards, the breath is comfortably stopped for a certain time, which is called kumbhak. Then the pranas are exhaled or taken downwards. The process is called rechak, and then breath is again stopped there or kubhak is applied. It is pertinent to mention here that the natural flow of pranas should not be altered forcefully or without proper guidance; otherwise, it disturbs the whole bodily mechanism. Further, these techniques should be followed by physical inhalation and exhalation of pranas without applying kumbhak for certain months in the beginning, viz., Anuloma viloma Pranayam. It is pertinent to mention here that Mantra Aum encapsulates this purification technique automatically, and in such cases there is no need for separate nostril exercises unless specifically required for fulfilling certain bodily balance.

Other Pranayam techniques: The pranayama techniques are mostly applied to operate pranas at specific energy centres, viz., for Manipura chakra (kapalbhati, Agnisar, and Nauli kriya) and for Anahata chakra (bhastrika pranayama), whereas ujayi pranayama is for throat chakra.

Padmaasan, Siddhasana, and Vajraasana: These asanas should be mastered so that our spine remains in excellent position and be ready for all physical, mental, and spiritual experiences. Pertinent to mention here that all spiritual development is dependent upon strong cerebrum, cerebellum, and backbone. So we must always work to keep them in excellent condition.

Anjali Mudra and Gyan Mudra: May also be applied during yoga practices along with Asanas for proper flow of energy in the body.

One must also walk for certain miles regularly, as it activates all bodily mechanisms. It encapsulates proper activity or functioning of all cells or organs of the body, for proper metabolism, for proper blood and prana flow inside the body, and also to improve our concentration. Thus, it is the easiest way to attune with one's body, mind, and self. Many yogis include this in their routine habits as part of meditation kriyas.

c). Eternal Happiness

Our true nature is joy and bliss. We, as human beings, are also no exception. We always seek pleasure and avoid pain. People are always seen creating a room for pleasurable things even out of their busy schedules. Everyone has their own approach to seeking happiness. Happiness indeed makes us feel lively and helps us embrace the joys associated with life. However, while going deep into it, we can observe that the definition of happiness is different for everyone. It indeed depends upon one's awareness level and the mental state to which he belongs. Thus, happiness for one may not be the same as for another, or it may also be possible that the other person may see it otherwise.

More concisely, for most people, the meaning of happiness lies in physical pleasure borne out of sense organs. They feel overwhelmed when they engage in activities that satisfy their instincts. They work on the philosophy of eating, drinking, and being merry. However, their source of happiness soon dissipates as they seldom care for nourishing their body and are solely governed by instincts that only enervate them of all energy and vigour ultimately.

Then next on the ladder are such persons who feel happy by conserving and channelling their energies. Such persons would feel happiness while gaining strength and vigour. Such people resort to physical exercises, yoga, pranayama, martial arts, etc. to gain strength and vigour. Such people enjoy phases of happiness more readily than people on the lowest rung.

Then come the people who find happiness while getting closer to nature. They learn art skills, which may comprise poetry, sketching, gardening, singing, adventure, etc. In this, the people attune their energies to nature and thus receive guidance and strength from the natural cycle.

Next come such people who find happiness in literary works. Such people are intellectuals and seek happiness through doing intellectual work.

The real pursuit of happiness lies in selfless work. When we do certain good for others, we feel happiness as we are all united as the same soul, and by serving others, we indeed serve ourselves.

Again, we feel happiness when we live a balanced life and thus are not deviated towards any one aspect of life fully. When we fully deviate towards any single aspect, then that aspect in turn demands all our consciousness and energy. Thus, we should live a life in such a way that it satisfies all the aspects of life. **Dr. Kewal Krishna Ji Maharaj once told that the reason for all the vikaaras is Abhaav (insufficiency).** It is to fulfil this Abhaav that this life comes into being. So if we can fine-tune every aspect of life by nourishing them optimally, then we feel fulfilled and satisfied, and that will be the real happiness indeed.

Thus, it may be considered that our happiness is a play of our awareness and our energy level. People who have high energy always engage more in this pursuit of happiness, as they have vast potential to absorb things in themselves and thus feel happiness in fulfilling their desires. Thus, energy in its purest form is all bliss, and when this energy unites to its source or consciousness, then it takes the form of eternal bliss. As we move higher in the ladder through both developing our energy prospects and gaining consciousness, the more permanence we feel in our happiness pursuits. At one time we start to belong with our true nature or soul, whose nature is eternal bliss, and as we may be able to uplift ourselves, the happiness and sadness that belong to the mortal body would not affect us, and thus we feel all blissful. After realising our full potential through amalgamation of mind with soul, we then feel the ultimate happiness, which is independent of time and space and thus regarded as eternal bliss. Thus, we must always try to realise ourselves so that we may experience this exalted state of eternal bliss, which is a quality of the soul. However, to move upward on this ladder, we must first develop the qualities of patience, compassion, sympathy, and empathy towards our fellow beings. If we belong with others and establish unbounded love for them, then we receive infinite bliss, as we in reality are the same, and when we expand ourselves with a love bond, then we experience a lot of happiness and joy rather than if we dwell in isolation. Further, knowledge and sacrifice also deepen the level of our awareness, and as we step deeper into our consciousness, we bathe in the eternal bliss that flows when we become part and parcel of truth.

Although these are the general pursuits of happiness, people are seldom found in one particular rung but are a mix of such pursuits, which in turn defines their personality types. This in turn

creates their unique identity based upon time and space.

In pursuit of happiness, the story of Yajnavalkya and Maitereyi as narrated in the Brihadaranyaka Upanishad needs a special reference here: -

The great sage Yājñavalkya was going to enter into the life of renunciation, the last phase of life (the four phases being Dharma, Artha, Kama, and Moksha). Before taking to the final stage of life, the sage called his consorts Maitreyi and Kātayāni to divide his property between them."

At this, Maitreyi thought at once that if his master is distributing all his accumulated material wealth and property so happily, then he must be receiving certain higher good of life.

So getting amazed with the offer, Maitreyi queried, "If this wealth is going to make me fulfilled throughout life, if not, then what is it that would make us perpetually happy and satisfied?"

"No," replied Yājñavalkya. "You cannot be perpetually happy by acquiring all the material wealth and property.

Yājñavalkya was highly pleased with this query and

told her the secret behind why we can't be perpetually happy by possession of all material endowments."

Happiness is the outcome of a transformation that takes place in the mind on account of an imagined connection of the mind with the object that is desired and possessed. Thus, happiness is not the condition of the object that is possessed. It is a condition of the mind and is based upon temporal arrangement (based upon time).

The desirability of the object is, again, a condition of the mind. The mind is a pattern of consciousness. A particular arrangement of consciousness in space and time may be said to be a mind, whether it is a human mind or otherwise. This particular arrangement of consciousness is naturally finite. So, the finitude of the mind becomes a source of restlessness to the mind as it tries to seek completeness. So, the mind tries to grab objects that it imagines to have characteristics that are the counterparts of what it feels it has lost.

The love that we feel in respect of an object is the love that we feel towards ourselves, which is based upon perfection and completeness of being. It is not merely a love for the object. The mind does not want an object; it wants completeness of being. That is what it is searching for. Thus, when it appears that the thing may complete us, then mind hankers after that object in order to experience the same. Through the perception of an object that appears to be its counterpart, there is a sudden feeling that fullness is going to come, and there is satisfaction even in the perception of that object. Thus, the mind tries to possess those things in hope of attaining ultimate satisfaction.

Again, when we feel incomplete in ourselves, we are unhappy; when we feel complete, we are happy. The sense of lack of something arises because there is a propensity for things in our mind due to a lack of completeness of being. When we get attracted towards something based upon our inclination, we expect that those things are going to fulfil the vacuum created in our mind. Till we do not possess those things, we keep thinking or craving for such things. But as soon as we get those things, our inclination shifts to yet other things.

Further, our idea regarding fulfilment or completeness of being keeps changing as we rise in the process of evolution. We cannot have one particular thing today and be happy forever. That is not possible, because the mind cannot rest in one condition and keep changing the idea of completeness based upon its understanding of life. It cannot rest because there is evolution. Pertinent to mention here that a person cannot become fully satisfied till it attains complete realisation of self. Thus this abhaav (lack of completeness) becomes his biggest obstacle, or vikara. **Thus the man's continuous journey is from incompleteness to completeness of being. The quest for knowing the senses (physiological knowledge) shifts to the understanding of mind and intellect (psychological knowledge), then about the soul (spiritual attainments), and then to God realisation (cosmic knowledge). Till then, the person cannot**

make a permanent halt in any situation, and it is only when he has a complete understanding of things that the mind ultimately comes to a standstill or immerses in the divine thought where it experiences eternal bliss and complete satisfaction.

So, our idea of the counterpart of the finitude (a sense of limited existence) of a mind is caused by the desirability of an object felt due to a limited view of reality based upon a particular condition (depending upon time and space). After maintaining proximity with such things, the mind assumes that it will make it complete', and wishes to assimilate such things as soon as possible and make them a part of its being.

Further, everything external is subject to change, and with the attainment of desired objects, the fear of losing them also starts looming (due to the operation of space and time). Thus, even if the mind settles at certain states, it is not permanent, and thus it obstructs the mind from feeling perpetual happiness and satisfaction. That is why this world is a sorrow, and it shall be a sorrow. There shall be a perpetual effort on the part of people to grab objects and try to enjoy them. But they cannot enjoy them. There can only be a mere appearance of enjoyment, not real enjoyment.

Yājñavalkya says nothing external can give you happiness. For the desire of the infinite, which is the self, everything appears to be desirable. Here, the word ātman is to be understood in the sense of the totality of being.

"O, Maitreyī, it is the ātman that is to be beheld; it is the ātman that is to be known; it is the ātman that is to be searched for; it is the ātman which is to be heard about; it is the ātman which is to be thought in the mind; it is the ātman which is to be meditated upon. There is nothing else worthwhile thinking, nothing else worthwhile possessing, because nothing worthwhile exists other than this."

"If you can grasp the significance of what this ātman is, you have known everything, and then you have possessed everything; you have become all things. There is nothing left to desire afterward. And if this is not to be achieved, what is going to be your fate? That which is not 'you' cannot be possessed by you. That which is not 'you' really, cannot be a property of yours. That which is not 'you' cannot be with you always. Therefore, it shall leave you. But why do you cry if anything goes away and there is bereavement, loss, etc.? It is quite natural to lose them; it is exactly as things ought to be. Things that are outside you do not belong to you; therefore, it is no use crying over them.

Eternal bliss is the quality of our soul. We are searching for it in the outside world. To satisfy this highest need, we have filled our lives with incessant desires. But nothing, irrespective of its lucrativeness, is fulfilling the most basic need of self. This is because we are looking for the right thing at the wrong place. We can get the requisite thing only from the place to which it belongs. A musk deer who looks after a heavenly scent all around but could not find it. This is because he never came to understand that the fragrance indeed belongs to him and is coming from within. So is the case with us. If we once settle at our place and get reunited with ourselves, then we automatically experience the everlasting state of eternal bliss from within. These are only the layers of ignorance that surround the soul, which are restricting the self from experiencing this state. The mind, being oblivious to self, looks for it in the external world, and till it does not delve within that, he never gets introduced to its true identity and never experiences the state of eternal happiness.

It has been observed that we are attracted to things not merely based on their outer appearance but because there is a proclivity within us for those things or persons. Our proximity to them gives us momentarily a feeling of completeness and fulfilment. Thus we embrace them and feel happiness while making proximal distance with them. However, every outer aspect is subject to decay, and if we overly attach to them, then it becomes the cause of our sorrows. Sometimes, due to setbacks caused by separation, we question the cosmic plan and start doing things haphazardly to show our will over nature. In this context, we have to learn that nature does not work on our whims and fancies and works only as per divine plan. If nature gives us something, then it is fruitful for us, and if it takes away something from us, it is again fruitful to us. Nature is the essence of the divine and fulfils the work of survival of the divine plan. It is the consort of Shiva, which is the consciousness attuned with universal laws. However, this consciousness is achieved when we fully realise our potential in all aspects of life, viz., physical, mental, intellectual, and spiritual. This indeed corresponds to the state of Brahman, where we experience Sat Chit Anand state of being. So we must try to attain this state where we become complete in ourselves and experience everlasting peace and bliss within ourselves.

Is there any end to ever-increasing demands from our lives? We have overburdened our lives with desires and cravings. These desires and wants never leave us settled, even for a second. Thus, we never get satisfied in our lives because of an imbalance created by such endless wants and desires. We also fear losing our limited identity, which only comprises material things, and desire to always make proximity with our loved ones. As we feed this limited identity day in and day out, it starts to expand infinitely, and thus this false identity always restricts us from merging with our source, and we always remain engrossed in fear of losing the identity to which we identify. The objects that belong to this misunderstood identity when enhanced give us momentary happiness and when depleted cause sorrow.

Thus this cycle of happiness and sorrow repeats through construction and devastation till we recognise ourselves as separate from the cosmos. When we surrender our limited self to ultimate divine reality and understand that we are its part and parcel, then we start to dwell in its lap and always get ready to experience life, but our consciousness always dwells in the infinite. Thus, when we can establish our divine link, we realise ourselves to be immortal and thus bestowed with eternal happiness in the form of divine grace or cosmic energy. This dissipates all our fears and sorrows as we start to experience ourselves as part and parcel of vast reality and not an object dependent upon time and space for its survival.

Our quality of life depends upon the quality of giving. We are interdependent upon each other for our happiness. Inward happiness is not some entity that we get through our efforts. It is the byproduct of patience and satisfaction. Satisfaction is bestowed when we live in harmony with our body, mind, and soul inward and in harmony with our fellow beings and other living creatures outside. Patience is bestowed when we can well regulate our thoughts, attitudes, and behaviour and do not lose temperament in various conditions imposed by time and space. However, for patience, resilience is to be first developed. Knowledge is the cornerstone in the pursuit of happiness. Through knowledge, we can make a difference between real and unreal and get acquainted with our true spirit, and through sacrifice, we only accept what is real and belong to ourselves. Surrender to Universal cosmic force is the real source of eternal happiness. Those who live for themselves are very small indeed in comparison to those who live as a part of a universal whole. Lastly, those are the happy beings who treat others in the same way they themselves want to be treated, as the same soul pervades all human beings.

10. Circle of Nature

Ramesh impressed upon his friends that we are on a sacred journey from living a limited life of individual consciousness to attaining supreme consciousness of being, where we also enlighten others while finding our own way. Further, he told his friends that we have many aspects of life out of which we have attained higher consciousness in certain aspects, while in others we are still striving to attain perfection. Based upon it, we have learnt certain characteristics and values that make us unique. But this uniqueness is short-lived, as we are constantly changing. So our focus should be towards attaining a universal understanding of being so that we seize to belong to limited awareness of body and instead become soul, which is complete, un-destructible, and ever blissful.

He further apprised me that we all have our past. Our past tells much about our life instances and the characteristics we imbibed as a result. For this reason, nobody in his life gains anything undeservingly. For becoming successful, we should be in harmony with our past. Our past should not elude us but give us a further way. We should not be entrapped in certain past events but should be free in letter and spirit.

Nature never bestows anything upon us till we have not aligned our consciousness with natural phenomena. We grow in each aspect and come closer to reality. Those who are possessed by only worldly things never come across their true nature. We all have our journey, our own experiences, and our leanings, based upon which we have some definite understanding of life. The deeper our awareness, the better we understand the different aspects of life.

Ramesh had long remembered how his friend Lokesh had strong imprints with nature. He used to dwell alongside nature in hilly regions and spent his whole childhood there. While dwelling amongst nature, he learnt the strong basis for the survival of life and also developed strong existential skills. Worthwhile to mention here that we exist in multiple dimensions. These are the physical plane, mental plane, and spiritual plane. Our existence at a universal level leads us towards immortality and depicts the nature of the soul, which is imperishable, indestructible, and everlasting, which corresponds to Sat, or permanent existence or life. Sat here denotes the truth, which is based upon the survival principle from which this whole world emanates.

Similarly, Sukhnandan was also fond of exploring nature. He had visited many places and hill resorts where he used to converse with people belonging to different regions and thereby adapt to the culture of different regions and follow their habits. Due to his proximity with nature, he developed a great sense of music, taste, social skills and etiquette, knowledge of different cultures, and understanding of the behaviour of people, etc., so he started embracing his nature and finding joy and love from it. This also leads one to another quality of soul, which is universal love and eternal bliss. Since it is the quality of the soul, for attaining this state one need not belong to any external state or maintain proximity with any place or person. It is the quality of the soul and sprouts from within, which in turn redeems all worries, stresses, and strains of life.

Ramesh himself had always remained close to nature. Indeed, nature had always been his closest friend. Ramesh was fond of starting his day with a morning walk in the nearby hills. He had spent his whole childhood embracing and exploring the nature goddess. Indeed, it has also bestowed him with many characteristics. It made him adventurous, creative, poetic, and alike. Due to the initiation of his life amidst nature, he also developed a deep understanding of nature and also about his being or self. When we completely grasp all concepts of life, then we attune ourselves with universal consciousness, where we understand and attune ourselves with all universal laws. This leads us near the seed of our creation, and through gaining cosmic intelligence, we understand divine and divine plans bit by bit. After having an understanding of all aspects of life, we finally surrender before the great will of God, whose indivisible part we are, and thereby immerse ourselves in the godly consciousness.

If we look at animals and plants, we see that they follow a fixed pattern related to all activities of their life, starting from sleep, eating, procreating, taking care of their health, and thus following the cycle of nature. But I don't know why human beings follow each other blindly, and in the race they forget to maintain balance with nature. This speaks highly about how they greatly misuse the mind bestowed on them, which other creatures are devoid of.

What else can nature do for us when it has provided us with all the prospects of life? Moreover, we never feel aloof while in its lap. How selfish a person would become if he still forgets about nature's infinite blessings and leaves it in his turn to chase some doom's paradise. A person is not leaving nature in that case; he is leaving the healthy conditions of his life indeed. Nature helps us nourish our individual aspects of being and takes our lives to higher states of consciousness. Simply, it provides us with a universal understanding of life. As we gain in our understanding and move towards deeper consciousness, we come closer to our universal identity of Brahm or Brahman. It is due to ignorance that we start thinking of ourselves as physical bodies and forget about our divine attributes, viz. Sat chit Anand, which is the quality of the self or soul.

a) Life is an examination

We are all exposed to life as per our understanding, and we may encounter difficulties based upon the challenges that we accept. Based upon it, we may also have different experiences of life. Further, the more difficult the exam is, the more it demands our ability and concern. However, while discovering our innate potential to deal with the situation, we may get near to ourselves, in which lies our core strength. Our infallible faith in ourselves and the supreme Lord helps us pass the tests of time. We may not know what we are testing for in life, but once we are ready to accept the challenge of life, then God intervenes in between and helps us cross all the hurdles. He comes to us in many forms to help us get through the problems of life.

During every moment, we have been tested for understanding of life. Life is spread like sheaths, where when we overcome one situation, the very next falls in front of us. The situation also tests our potency and our readiness to deal with certain aspects of life. In this world, nobody can be raised to higher standards until he is not worthy of it. Sometimes, when, with the guru's grace, a certain person climbs the ladder of evolution, the responsibility for his corrected behaviour lies with the mentor.

Many of us might have realised that life repeats the same situation in front of us in different forms. The unprepared ways of life thus keep haunting us till we don't learn the correct behaviour to deal with them. So in a way, life, through its pitfalls, guides us in the proper way to deal with various situations in life. Every situation develops our psyche and our absorption power for things happening around us. **When certain situations in different forms come across us more readily, it means that the situation is preparing us to deal with frustration and our ego involvement in that particular situation.** On the contrary, if we neglect any situation in life, then we remain oblivious about that aspect of life. The same situation comes to us and haunts us till we do not learn to deal with it effectively. This whole universe is engulfed with specific knowledge of things. When we surrender before situations and try to learn their basis, then the whole knowledge related to it comes to us and helps us in further finding our way. But when we neglect any aspect of our being and try to escape particular situations, then unconsciously we try to repel the learning associated with it and thus create a vacuum in our lives that resists the learning associated with that particular situation. Thus unconsciously we attract more of such situations to come across us and deviate us from our path due to the vacuum in our lives. Thus, only a person who has crossed all the situations successfully is bestowed with the characteristics to win over life. Only such a person can be of use to others who have crossed the hurdles of life and are thus prepared to serve others through their emotions and wisdom.

Also, nature never bestows us with higher consciousness states till we are not ready for it. If we somehow make access to a certain higher state for which we are not prepared, then we can disturb the natural cycle of life as well as end up doing injustice to those who relate to us. Thus nature blocks our way till we do not learn the right approach to life. Till we cultivate the art of self-absorbing things by developing a deeper consciousness, we may never be allowed for a deeper experience of life. Finally, we become one with a universal reality where nothing conflicts with anything. What we receive is a continuous flow of consciousness where no conflict in thoughts, actions, or speech remains with any other particle of consciousness. In other words, when the mind starts to flow freely even during conflicting situations, it achieves a harmonious state, and thus, in that scenario, the mind merges with universal consciousness, or the soul.

If we look at the world, we can see that there is a definite order, and nothing works on free will but on higher or universal principles. If any system deviates from this principle, then it automatically slips down from the origin farther and farther and thus enjoys lesser will. The system that does not fully work on universal principles is faulty, and the farther we deviate, the more faults we may possess, and vice versa.

11. Nature opens its way only to the deserving (overactivity leads to chaos and disruption).

Only when we follow the right path does nature open the way for us. If we do not have the requisite characteristics, viz., moral, mental, and spiritual traits, and still try to elevate ourselves by performing a lot of austerities/penance, then it will only create tension in our bodies and minds. Doing this would also disrupt the natural equilibrium and cause devastation and chaos due to overactivity. We would thus unconsciously indulge in various vikaras borne out of unregulated thoughts and energy due to the over-excitation of our mind. All this happens without us having any control over our minds. This only leaves us to reap its result afterwards.

To go deeper, nature works on certain phenomena. When energy flows without any disruption, then it does not cause any harm. This happens only when all centres of energy are well activated. However, when enormous energy flows in lower centres, then according to the rule, an energy transition takes place where energy alters its state and thereby flows into higher centres. However, if the higher consciousness energy centres are not yet realised or activated owing to a lack of proper understanding, then it only causes turbulence in the body and mind, which then ends up in vikaras, or psychosomatic disorders.

It so happens that when a certain element excites beyond a certain level, it has to change its state, but devoid of realisation of the next state, it only rotates in its initial state with higher momentum and energy, which is required only for the next level. As it is not able to acquire this higher level, it only causes turmoil in the previous state. This can be understood through understanding the core concept of phase transition in particles or the process of sublimation. If the system is not ready for this transition, then it would only cause disruption and chaos like a pressure cooker. Thus, in the given scenario, we either require to make way for the next phase or slower the rate of reaction in the initial state through the cooling effect (to counter the effect of excessive heat and thereby momentum). In this regard, we may also increase the flow of tamas or inactivity to cope with excessive heat or energy.

Sometimes, it is also seen that the people directly resort to higher frequencies for which the body and mind are not yet prepared. In such scenarios, the person most likely ends up damaging their nerve tissues or creating an abnormality of the mind. So one must not jump on such states haphazardly based upon hearsay or upon excitement but should approach only when a person is conscious about such states and has developed one's psyche and bodily capacity to withstand such frequencies.

Based upon this phenomenon, our behaviour and psyche are largely affected. This is why people on the sacred journey sometimes deviate from their path. They never understand why they have deviated from their path and think that some unknown power is stopping them from treading their path, and thus they curse their fate or almighty for the disruption created in their life. They also seldom realise that their inability to transform or lack of development of optimum consciousness level is indeed impeding their self-growth and causing disruption and chaos in their lives.

Due to a lack of full consciousness or inner capacity, their energies are not fully channelled. Thus keeping this instability of mind and body into consideration, where a tremendous amount of energy is called into action without first developing an optimum state of consciousness, all saints always advise to go slow in the spiritual path. This happens when we steadily and cautiously gain consciousness and also develop the capacity of body and mind to withstand higher frequencies associated with such higher consciousness levels. They also advise us to surrender to a realised saint (who is one with universal spirit) as well as to universal spirit/Paramatma so that we continue to receive divine grace and guidance in our sacred journey.

Pertinent to mention here that surrendering to the universal spirit also means that we follow the truth or universal laws in any given condition, and all our actions are devoted to the universal cause. It is to be understood that universal consciousness always has a deeper impact on our mind and intellect, and when we obey the universal commandments through self-surrender, then it always helps us with its divine grace and right direction of life. It is to be further understood that we are connected with the divine, and every aspect of our being is first expressed at higher dimensions, and then it comes to our mind or intellect in the form of thoughts or physical impulses. This can be understood through developing understanding about the law of quantum entanglement, which states that every manifestation at the gross level has origin in an unmanifested portion of life at the causal level, which can then be regarded as the cosmic womb or Hiranya Garbha.

The other way around, when we do not surrender to the ultimate reality and do work based upon our whims and fancies, then in a way we sometimes disturb the natural order due to plain ignorance, and thus nature being the essence of the almighty intervenes in between. It stops us from our path by maligning our intellect, which in turn pollutes our karmas. Thus it entangles us in the cycle of karma till the right approach is not followed. It has to be understood that all consciousness levels require certain characteristics to be emulated, and if any vikaras contrary to them exist, then such levels can never be realised. That's why all spiritual masters always advise controlling vikaras in all their forms at once.

(through proper understanding) if a person wants to tread the field of spirituality or, in that case, wishes to lead an ideal life.

In this sacred journey called life, we must have full surrender before the almighty, whose essence we are, so that we may be able to follow the right path after receiving true divine guidance. Through following the path of truth, we open our vast spiritual potential and receive the divine grace, which then erases all layers of ignorance enveloped around our true being so that we can shine as a self after realising our true nature.

a) Order and discipline are the keys.

Based upon all the constituents of life, nature has maintained a specific order, and this order is itself conserved by cosmic force. When something becomes disorderly, it withers away. So for sustenance and dissolution of life, we must be aware of such order. Nobody is allowed to surpass this order. Even the holy spirits and divine forces are subject to such laws. Vedantins knew this as Rita, or cosmic order.

From atoms to big galaxies, everything has a specific order based upon their energy and consciousness. As we move upwards on this ladder, the more perfection we would notice, and vice versa. The energy is distributed among them in the form of quantum. So there is a threshold required for moving from one quantum to another. At the higher dimensions, everything works on definite principles. Things do not move with our emotions or concern, but they work purely on reason and rationale. However, emotions are required to channel our energy in the way we want, but that does not mean that we would be able to achieve higher dimensions of life even when our emotions are confining us towards lower dimensions of life. If energy is stuck somewhere, it does not mean that there is a lack in our efforts. It simply means that we are still not fully attuned to certain frequencies (either higher or lower) and are required to put our efforts into harmonising such aspects of our lives. Many people put their energies at higher dimensions, but devoid of true understanding of various aspects of life, they fall prey to their misunderstanding or ignorance and finally settle on compromised life spheres. Due to their energies vibrating at lower frequencies, they may also attract the negative forces to dwell in, which in turn causes disease and discomforts of life. It is pertinent to mention here that energy in its purest form is all organised. So if we maintain cleanliness and order in our lives, then we are creating more room for energy to come in. However, where there is entropy or disorderliness, the energy gets stuck and cannot move freely. So even if a person is very conscious and enlightened, even if he is not following order and discipline, then the energy remains divorced from him. So that this energy flows seamlessly, there is a need for discipline and order.

Discipline is the cornerstone of whatever we get in life. If we do everything in sync with time, then nature will grace us with the choicest blessings. The more disciplined a person becomes, the more one evolves in life.   Knowledge is disgraced if we cannot put it into action. Through routinely following a discipline of life, we become more ordered, and thus, as per a universal phenomenon, we are bestowed with incessant energy, which further helps us achieve the objects of our concentration or goals of life. Pertinently, the energy in its purest form is devoid of knowledge and, when aided with consciousness, gives us prospects to realise the various dimensions of life, be they physical, vital, mental, intellectual, or purely bliss. In this scenario, consciousness is lame but has eyes, i.e., it can show the way, and energy is blind, though it has legs, i.e., it can move. So in order to reach their destination, consciousness sits on the shoulders of energy. In this way, consciousness tells the way, and energy takes them to their destination following the commands of consciousness.

12. Empowering self to lead its way

Only the person who follows the truth in any given condition gets acquainted with their true self. Self plays a pivotal role in deciding the fate of life as it has complete control over all three dimensions of life, viz., past, present, and future. It always directs the mind to follow a wise course. It always guides it to the true way of life. It protects the mind and body from unforeseen problems. However, the mind seldom listens to this inner voice and thus repents things after the situations have their harsh effect on life. To truly follow the inner voice, a person should be free from vikaras and unregulated thoughts and also from overly attachment to things or people. When the mind is free from scrap material, then one's self becomes visible and commands all aspects of life. The self becomes predominant as one understands the universal principles and starts following them, and when one's intentions are pure and aligned with truth. When the self remains so attached to the mind, then it does not channelise and direct the mind on the right track. It instead remains a mere spectator and sees the mind indulging in various vikaras and feels happy with the momentary happiness of the mind.

Self-realisation here means self is taking the lead role and channelling all aspects of life. It also means complete surrender. of the mind to self and, in turn, obeying all universal laws and thus becoming part and parcel of the divine plan. It comes with fully realising the fact that not even a particle can move without the greater will of the almighty.

a) Encountering Death

From infinite consciousness there dwells a space for unlimited awareness. For every fragmentation of this consciousness, the corresponding awareness also shifts and is spread across different energy levels along with their definite experience. Thus, life is a temporary transition from infinite to finitude, where we experience different dimensions of single reality and create awareness about manifested and unmanifested aspects of divine.

Life is a continuous stream of consciousness that is spread across a definite space and depending upon a specific time. As this space moves farther, it lags in consciousness and so in energy. Thus, when we gain consciousness, we may also realise our potential and thus have a better experience of life, and vice versa. Depending upon level of consciousness, we also have two extremities of positive force and corresponding negative force. Here positive force connotes consciousness, negative force connotes corresponding energy level, and so on. It is pertinent to mention here that when energy flows towards consciousness, it is constructive, and vice versa.

Further, it is not always that we encounter positivity when performing righteous actions. Dr. Kewal Krishna Ji once said that in the path of righteousness, be ready for hell as well. With every positivity created, there dwells the room for negativity as well. Thus, to counter this negativity in all its forms is realisation of self. During the deeper phases of life, we encounter these negativities, which are dwelling within due to our faulty actions caused by misconceptions. It is a must first understand the basis of negativity so that it is corrected. As it involves ablution of all mental misconceptions and immersion of mind into truth, it is like encountering death.

Ramesh always led with a strong drive to realise himself. He always tried to follow the truth in all given conditions. Due to this, he always invited uncalled-for miseries in life due to illusory forces created by his own mind. He always surrendered before truth, and truth in turn helped him to cross every obstacle that came across him. When we surrender before any other force except truth, then we temporarily manage for the time being to get shelter/relief from our wrong karmas. It is just like taking a painkiller for an underlying disease without ever trying to find the roots of the disease. But with passage of time and due to ignorance, we perform so many wrong deeds that we reach the point from where we never have our comeback and thus become prey of circumstances and time. However, when we perform our actions in light of truth, then our lives get tuned in accordance with universal laws, which in turn attract cosmic divine energy to pour in. It does not mean that we disregard the divine forces, but simply means that we must first understand the universal laws in light of truth, and only then that we may bow before other aspects of divine reality for shelter and grace other than divine cosmic force. As we get attuned to truth, we work purely on the basis of reasoning at all levels of consciousness, viz., body, mind, and spirit, satisfied with nothing other than what is truth. When we harmonise all these levels, then we become one in thoughts, words, and deeds, and cosmic energy starts to flow within us uninterruptedly. Thus, whatever we think becomes true because we become part and parcel of divine reality.

Where one has to surrender all that he has, viz., mind, intellect, and ego, before the cosmic force and become an observer, we instead perform actions solely recognising ourselves to be individual entities. When we face defeat afterwards due to wrong cognition, we then become exhausted and fearful.

This is the last test of illusion or the first step of wisdom. Those who are one with the almighty sail through it, and those who believe in their individual capacity get lost. Individuality has to give way to universality. If we had a look into epics, we would understand how the strong forces of individuality are encountered by universal heads. Here the role models of Dharma like Bhagwaan Krishna and Rama uphold the universal principles, whereas on the other hand always lie the forces of individuality like Ravana and Duryodhana and their supporters who became threats before

Dharma, or the universal order of the Cosmos. Thus Individuality always gives way to universality.

Due to illusory forces created by duality of mind, Ramesh also once encountered dark phases of life. He tried to counter the evil forces through all the gathered energy and confidence, but he seems to fall short before them. Due to exhaustion of energy, he also started feeling frightened and defeated. But nevertheless, he did not feel hopeless. He had indomitable faith in the almighty and righteousness, whom he had followed throughout his life. It was indeed his only possession, which he valued throughout life over material possessions. He only knew that consciousness has to prevail over the power notwithstanding its intensity and hold (consciousness and power both belong to supreme). So with all consciousness, he invoked the divine Mother in all its forms to give him thrust to boldly face the dark phases of life. He long cherished the words of his mentor, who once told him that no worries if you can't see God; the almighty indeed sees you. Due to his undiluted trust and infallible grace received from the Almighty, he learnt the deepest secrets of life and was introduced to the Shakti cult. He indeed had to encounter death in its last phase of ignorance.

Shakti is both an unmanifested and manifested part of divine reality. To encounter the ill forces, the primordial divine power requires to be realised from within. So, in order to get attuned to the feminine aspect, Ramesh invoked the mother. goddess. With pure devotion and dedication, Ramesh could be able to overcome his shortcomings and the curse of negativity, which suddenly turned into Ramesh's greatest boon, which further helped him to sail through the ocean of life by getting a complete understanding of life.

We do not get things till we have not sacrificed the things to which we are overly attached. Overly attached causes pain and agony and needs to be overcome. Emotions, when effectively encountered, become our strength. This world is merely a dream-like state. Here, everything that is happening is merely an illusion. Sometimes we may feel that this is utter stupidity if we are so involved in life that we break our connection with the divine for keeping proximity with things when everything that happens is because of grace received from the divine.

Our body (gross, subtle, and causal) is composed of five elements, and these elements always have an effect on our psyche. Till every element and corresponding chakra is not well activated, we become prey to various illusory forces despite all positivity. Activating chakras or energy centres has to do with gaining adequate conscious experience of each aspect of reality. Until then, the negative or illusory forces of Tantra (chemical reactions), Mantra (vibrations), and Jantra (mechanical instruments) may have an effect on us. We also need to direct our Pranic Shakti through the sushmana canal (lying on the backbone) in order to realise our full potential. To start with regular enchanting of aum would force pranas to enter the sushmana canal at Mooladhar and reach up to trikuti Madhya and then to the crown chakra after clearing all other chakras.   After this, the advanced mool kriyas (to and fro movement of prana and apana from Mooladhar to Sahastra Kamal Dal) and the "Hamsa" or "So Hum" techniques would suffice.

Pertinent to mention here that our mind is filled with filthy and base matter, and till all the scrap matter is cleared, we are unable to self-actualise ourselves and thus cannot vibrate at higher frequencies. Our minds cause much damage to us when governed by base instincts. It also attracts the negative vibrations to capture our awareness and thus impedes our growth. Further, our base or individual mind and emotions are governed by primordial divine power, and to clear the scrap, we invoke divine mother to clear our pathways in order to realise the truth. When we take ultimate refuge in Mother Goddess, it helps us to understand our real nature and attune our mind with it. Thus, our sole concern should be to understand Mother Nature and not to fulfil our incessant desires and wishes. When we surrender ourselves before the primordial divine force, then it embraces us with its pure love and also helps us find our way.

13. Bringing goodness into life

We seldom focus on ourselves. We remain engrossed in this world. We have our relatives to whom we belong. We want leisure time to enjoy our lives. We prefer material endowments over self-building. We prefer pleasurable over good. "The one who embraces the good or right meets with auspiciousness. But the one who chooses the pleasant is lost." Katha Upanishad.

We have to remember that all material endowments and relations have their charm only till this self-survives. The harsh reality of life is that when this self of ours downgrades, then nobody except the divine treads down to lift us. On the contrary, when this self-shines through performing the right deeds, then everybody tries to belong to us and feels proud by relating to us. In reality, no one emulates a looser, even if it has strong traits. Everybody looks for successful people because their trust and concern are also conditioned due to the fears encompassing their lives.

So we must understand this phenomenon, and rather than cursing others for their selfishness, we should focus on developing ourselves so that we can be of use to many. In actuality, the true wealth of a person lies in his character or the traits that he holds. We can earn material endowments again with our strong character, but if the person either does not possess the high traits or has lost such traits by indulging in wrong deeds, then such person would also lose their material endowments in due course of time.

Everything that a man gets in his life is what he truly deserves. We cannot receive even a penny if we have not strived for it. Thus, efforts should be such that they are directed towards accomplishing the goals of life. We cannot strive long if we are begging for others' grace. Even the luck that plays a predominant role in our lives has roots in our past efforts, whose fruits we receive in multiple ways. So the crux is that we should regularly work on ourselves and improve our lives so that a true direction is given to our lives.

Those people who always excel in their lives who treat themselves as trustees of the universal spirit. In reality, we owe this life to the divine, and to live it successfully, we must always remember that we are playing our roles and that, based upon it, our destiny will be decided. This way we can also remain free from the burden imposed by one's ego. The same principle also applies when we are serving in the form of an organisation. There too, we should understand that we are performing all actions on behalf of an organisation and are thus answerable. There are a few people who hold certain higher posts in their lives who start thinking of their subordinates as their slaves. Thus they have to repent for their misconception and faulty perception and thus can never tread the true path of life. They remain engulfed in this falsehood and remain confined to their limited selves only, as life never discloses itself before them fully.

People nowadays treat material endowments and healthy relations as success. However, understand that true success lies in being yourself. If you are doing the things as expected from you and that you are doing what is right without ever deviating by the charm of life, then in a way you feel a sense of completeness in your life, which also gives you real satisfaction and joy within. Thus, those persons who hanker after material endowments while neglecting their true inner selves never receive the divine grace, and they always feel the emptiness within despite possessing all the luxuries of life. The reason is that their life is devoid of their true self and that they are living a life of sensuality and outward charm. They must tread the spiritual journey to redefine their lives.

14. The law of attraction revisited

It has been observed that people generally crave one thing or the other. They put in a lot of effort into realising such states. Despite putting in so much effort, a person may seldom achieve such states, and even if he can get to that state, it is only momentarily, and with it carries a lot more sorrow than happiness. It is because we put so much effort into achieving certain states that we lose focus on other aspects of life and thus create an imbalance in our lives. This later on becomes the cause of our miseries. On the contrary, our goal should be to achieve equilibrium in life, which then leads towards self-development. When we focus largely on ourselves, then we are also bestowed with other necessities of life that are only meant for us as we rise in our ability. We always get things as per our wishes when we have balanced our energies within, but when we disturb the equilibrium, then the small obstacles of life also seem to be insurmountable due to a lack of requisite energy and consciousness.

Again, it has also been seen that when we crave anything in life, that craving becomes manifold due to our mind's processing and that it thus engrosses us to fulfil such desires and cravings. It thus deviates us from our concentration on our real selves and creates a false identity for us based on illusive thoughts. Indeed, it is the work of our mind to multiply them, thus making us restless to pursue those uncalled-for goals. We may find many people whose concentration is distracted towards all outside pursuits and worldly charms, but they are least focused towards allotted work. Such people fall on the lower ebb of evolution, or simply they may have retrogressed. Then, at the higher end of such a ladder, there are those people who are depicted to be much focused, but when encountered by certain vikara, they forget about their goals and get possessed by them. The early life of Tenali Rama depicts the former, and the encounter of Vishvamitra with Apsara Maneka depicts the latter. Thus we must all work to focus on our real nature and do allotted work sincerely and dedicatedly without getting distracted by the outer charm or getting in complete hold of one's vikara.

During life, we aspire for many things, and for them, we give our best. But sometimes it happens that irrespective of our efforts, we may not be able to get the things we desire. In those times we become so depressed and frustrated that we start cursing our luck and, with time, develop many other passions to keep aside our repressed feelings associated with our unfulfilled goals. Here we must realise that the purpose of our life is not solely to fulfil only one aspect of life but carries in its bosom many other aspects that together make life meaningful and purposeful. Even if we are fully able to realise one aspect of life, we may not feel happy and rather distressed if other aspects of life are not equally fulfilled. Thus, rather than craving to fulfil our desires and goals, we must try to put adequate efforts into realising those goals and, side by side, also look after other aspects to be   fulfiled.

When our efforts get fully ripened, we could be able to draw its fruit so easily, and as a blessing from nature.

What people call luck is also our accumulated efforts in life to which nature gives a certain direction. Believe that nature never does injustice to anyone. When others fail to appreciate your efforts, even then nature has all records of your holdings and intentions. It reverts to you at an appropriate time and gives everything back to you with dividends that you have put across it. Thus, always try to put in your best and be based upon righteousness so that when it comes back to you, you may not feel discomfort while holding it back.

15. Mismatch between the mental self and the ideal self

We are devoured by our expectations, as what we are living is not ideally true of us, and what is ideal for us has not taken root, or in simple terms, such qualities have not yet developed naturally within us. We are trying to impose conditions on us that are making our unconscious mind restless and in struggle for existence. When certain qualities naturally develop, then we are at ease with our nature, and that further helps to define ourselves ideally. So we don't wait for nature to take its course and try to jump onto the higher aspects of life without first realising those aspects of life and thereby getting control over them. Here we have not developed the optimum capacity for such qualities to persist and thus face resistance from the mind due to lack of harmony created in those states. Harmony is created when we are fully conscious about those aspects and when we have full energy for their realisation, not that we have a vacuum of it where energy and consciousness both lack. Thus, the mind becomes more restless when it is imposed with certain conditions for which it is not prepared. For this, we must first delve within and try to first understand our unique nature and develop bonhomie with it. Thereafter, we must inculcate traits conducive to withholding higher standards of life.

It has been seen on multiple occasions that we live a delusional life where our thoughts hamper us more than anybody could do. Take the example that you started thinking of yourself as an expert athlete when, in reality, you still need to learn certain skills necessary for becoming an expert, followed by adequate energy required for realising that state. If instead of improving your skills and working on your stamina, you maintain the status quo and think of yourself as an expert, then in all probabilities you would end up hurting yourself profusely. Thus we must know about our reality and should not hesitate to reconcile with our real state and thus carry ourselves further.

We can observe this in spiritual experience as well when people forget about their level of understanding and jump to meet extreme results, which only cause more trouble created by their minds. Certain people also cause so much tension to their bodies that they cannot bear the pressure and succumb. They assume that they are pure spirits that are detached from body and mind, whereas in reality they are attached at many levels, viz., bodily, mental, social, intellectual, moral, etc., which we really do. Before they unite with their spirit fully, they need to develop a thorough understanding of all these essential aspects of life and then strive for higher aspects of life only after harmonising the lower aspects of life.

For complete self-development, one's physical, mental, intellectual, and moral aspects should also be fully activated. Complete physical, mental, and intellectual development is also necessary to enhance our genetic capacity to adjust to energy phenomena that may partake in the realisation of self-potential. The development of self means nothing if the container that carries it, i.e., body, is cracked or not well prepared. Thus, we must nourish it regularly.

To give life a true direction, we must take recourse to divinity, and through help and guidance received from divine spirits, we must work tirelessly to achieve various goals in all dimensions of life. It is our prime duty to establish dharma through cultivating positivity in life and confronting the negativity present within and outside with all our might and faith in the divine. Till we have not realised ourselves completely, we always need help from divinity, and even after realising, we depend upon its grace.

16. Higher purpose in life

Life has been designed in a way that fulfils our desires and needs. The quality of our lives depends upon the targets and ideals that we embrace in our lives. Those whose lives are filled with higher purposes always welcome all the challenges of life. Whereas those who live on low ideals or those who just love to pass their lives never welcome tough life situations and bow before them at their very outset. Thus everything depends upon our schema. Our mind sees situations as per our mind's frame. However, those who accept such challenges have very high and purposeful lives as compared to those who hasten to tread life's path.

One thing to keep in mind is that life always sets before us in its multifold outlook. It is only up to us how deeply we can thrive. The more intense we are, the more quality we put up in our lives. Those who always live at the shore with the fear of drowning even in shallow water can never explore the possibilities of life. Those who go deep inside it, encountering life challenges with perseverance and preparation, always learn as well as explore new dimensions of life. Moreover, they also learn to overcome life's situations through gaining experience and learning the wise course.

Again, when we accept certain challenges of life, then automatically we gain confidence in ourselves, and our mental schema also expands, thereby welcoming new possibilities in life. This schema helps us overcome the untrodden mysteries of life and also helps us encounter our fear. Thus, we should always try to live up to our optimum capability and strength so that when we encounter new challenges in life, it helps us build ourselves further on.

We may see that when we live a purposeless life, then we may not be able to grow ourselves fully and realise ourselves up to our optimum strength. There is always a certain life pattern that seldom allows us to grow ourselves to our optimum capacity. So we need to stretch ourselves further to make room for our aspirations and goals if they are based upon higher ideals. Only then will we be able to channel our energy optimally, which helps us achieve perfection and one-pointed concentration.

Actually, when higher purpose is missing in our lives, then our life in turn attracts towards sensual passions, which in turn give only low meaning to our lives. On the contrary, when our concentration remains on a certain higher purpose, then these sensual passions automatically give way to living up to our higher ideals. Thus we must not pass our time but live it by giving concrete shape to our goals, daily, and giving our best so that life transforms itself in the best possible way and we may be able to see our life transforming in the manner we want it to be.

17. Do Karmas really need to be blamed?

We may always ponder as to whether karma creates trouble in our lives or whether the lack of knowledge along with illusion causes much havoc.

It has been seen that we readily blame our past karmas for everything that is happening in our lives. Indeed, it is true that karmas play a pivotal role in shaping our lives. But this karma should not be taken as a burden on us. It is also an opportunity to frame new events in our lives, irrespective of our past. However, due to clinging to our past habits, we continue to act mechanically based upon past impressions and seldom apply our faculties of mind and pure will to reframe our lives. Thus, due to a lack of knowledge vis-à-vis absolute will, we get stuck in a vicious cycle of past karmas, and seldom do we take things into our charge. Indeed, we need to take active control of our lives and make the best possible use of them. We must understand that we harness energy cycles around us that shape our lives. These energy cycles work both as individual quantum cells and also synergistically, where the higher centres may channel and control the lower ones. To make life vibrate at higher frequencies, we must try to become more active and conscious about reality. This is possible when we bring positivity into our lives by upholding the principles governing life. When we create positivity in our lives, we are propelled by the divinity, which in turn fills our lives to the brim. Thus, we can reach our goals more readily.

Negativity in turn blocks our way, and when it is created around us, even the things that seem easy become unsurmountable. It causes us to vibrate at lower frequencies, which in turn attracts like forces in our lives and thus makes our lives deplorable. In the same way, lust and other vices are also forms of negativity. It causes our energies to vibrate at lower frequencies, which ultimately enervates us of all vigour and strength.

Further, this negativity does not go on its own. To counter it, we need to improve our energy aura along with changing the bent of our mind to make a frame for positivity to take its course. It has been seen that it is easy to strive for excellence during the normal course of time. However, when negativity takes grip over our minds, it causes various ailments, both physically and mentally. At this juncture, it becomes cumbersome for us to alter our path to create room for optimism and positive growth. It is easy to fight demons outside, but it becomes very difficult to counter them inside of us because they have survived upon our weaknesses and our wrong approach towards life. Thus, to challenge self-created adversaries, we must be equipped with a strong desire for survival together with the right approach towards life. We must acquire the right knowledge of things through unbiased inquiry, and when we put our knowledge into our deeds, The rightful result always comes by. There is no evil around. If there is one, it is only our sheer ignorance, as we seldom realise our vast potential and breed the seeds of illusions, which in turn give rise to evil or negative karma. Thus we must reframe our karmas to whom we should nourish with optimum energy and consciousness.

Till we take our own responsibility, the forces of inertia, inactivity, or waywardness would remain to continue to haunt us, and if we do not find ourselves at fault, then we keep blaming our bad luck or past misdeeds for our helpless condition. Seldom would we realise that it is not our past karmas but our ignorance and illusion altogether with our misdeeds that is responsible for negative outcomes of life. Thus we need to wake from the deep slumber of ignorance and find our accurate position vis-à-vis the cosmos to enjoy eternal bliss and peace of mind.

There is a story of a sadhu who had reached the pinnacles of spiritual heights. However, due to a lack of complete faith, he fell prey to ignorance and got afraid of the heights. Due to this, the seeds of inertia fell upon the sadhu, and his consciousness became diluted, and thus his energy cycle also diminished to an abysmal low. Thus he forgets about himself and is engulfed in the world of Maya. He got caught there due to learnt helplessness, for if he had tried with full vigour he would have crossed the threshold at once. However, he continued to receive grace, but despite it, he remained clung to his past learnt fear and did not try to take charge of his life.

and thus could not even complete the distance of an inch required to realise himself fully. The problem was not some particular situation but his lack of complete surrender. He continued to search for the accurate situation to turn it into his fortune when he had indeed created the wrong scene due to fear of falling apart.

We indeed are beyond every situation. The thing is only to follow the truth in all given situations and thereby develop complete trust in the supreme sweet will of the almighty. However, we remain confined to our limited minds and try to keep things by our side even by flouting the universal laws or truth. Thus we remain a drop of water and cannot become one with the mighty ocean. Likewise, we become an individual mortal being and remain subject to individual laws, thus restricting universal or cosmic grace from falling upon us.

The person remains clung to the fear of the unknown and never steps into the untrodden path. Due to this, we even miss a lot of visible opportunities in life because we fear that some unknown power would take us under its control or that our past deeds would control our lives and not let us succeed. Due to this fear, we never try our best to get the situation under our control. We never put our best efforts and never cause the faculties of mind into full action. This energises us and becomes the biggest hurdle in our lives. This is true for every dimension of reality, be it physical, mental, intellectual, or spiritual.

One must try his to his fullest to keep oneself fully active. One must learn the true values of life, and one must be fully devoted to life's cause. One must also learn to see goodness and divinity in every aspect of life. One's heart should be filled with immense love and live a life one of gratitude towards God or the universal self. Truth should be predominant and guide one's way. This creates better outcomes in life, and this also enhances the quantum of knowledge about the self and its oneness with the divine source. Finally, one must learn the art of supreme surrender and leave the result to the cosmos. The universe never lets you go without the results that you indeed deserve. It gives you the things most suitable for you and also teaches you the right spirit to live life to its fullest.

18. Always try to be the best version of yourself.

We can't enjoy our life to the fullest till we have not realised ourselves fully. We may pass our time craving for one thing or another when we have better things to accomplish in this limited life. We have indeed better value than what we have put into our lives. We have shrunk ourselves due to our lame and unwanted desires. In the given circumstances, no one other than us can decide our fate.

We are not born to live a low life, but due to our narrow-mindedness, we may not be fully able to realise our vastness and what we are up to. When we fail to realise the value of our life, then others not only take control of it but also thereby direct our destiny and fate. So always take full charge of your life so that room for ignorance or illusion to dwell cannot make space. We must have our full development, be it physical, moral, intellectual, or spiritual. Only those who try to find out the value of life come up with fruitful results. When we attract life in all its facets, then it opens up before us in its true spirit. We must not live life in a cocoon but always try to adhere to universal laws and thus realise our full potential. When we deviate from our true path, then we get deluded by illusion, which only gives us dissatisfaction in all spheres of life as we deviate from reality.

One step we take in the right direction is followed by thousands of steps from the universe as a grace. This may be equated with the butterfly effect. So, when we get stuck somewhere fully and can't move, in that case just believe that if we take one small step with full vigour and determination, then that is enough to get us out of such an unwanted situation, as God's grace in the form of creating its infinite possibility would follow by.

Again, we are interdependent upon each other as we have descended from the same source. When we help someone find its ways, God shows us our own. Help the needy person and get helped by the universe. We have been designed to help each other find our way. When we don't help, then we remain bound to limited karmas, which create unlimited miseries. So we must embrace each other and help each other find the right way. We must first try to seek the path of truth and then rekindle others's paths. When one deviates from truth, it is only then that all the miseries of life start to take root. So we have to get along with the truth to live a blissful life. We can't escape from our reality anyhow. So we must be committed to being one with our true selves by accepting reality as it is and tuning one's self with it.

Sometimes it happens that we see darkness everywhere and there is hopelessness that remains. We feel that we are losing our race of life and that we have become helpless. Believe that during this phase of utter darkness, only a small light would do all the work. After darkness has its most impact, even a small ray of light overcomes it. In the pitch darkness, a little spark is enough to rekindle our way and shed the darkness. When we still strive even in utter despair, then this whole universe comes to our refuge as if the whole cosmos favours life over despair.

We are not a tiny entity but part and parcel of a cosmic whole. When we are overshadowed by darkness, we may forget our true identity and succumb to circumstances, but when we light a small candle of hope in our refuge, that event has an exponential effect. This is another law of nature that works on the principle of activity. **A small movement of our limb can force the whole universe to find its basis as it envisions life and vibrates with its frequency**. Thus we must embrace the principle of activity in utter despair as well. **When we call higher frequencies of life into action through our infallible trust and hopefulness, then lower vibes corresponding to inactivity or death automatically subside and give way to higher will**. Thus, always be hopeful and always hold your head high in all circumstances to live a valuable life one of control.

19. Meeting the Ends of Life

Ramesh explained all the concepts related to Atma or self to his friends Lokesh and Sukhnandan. They get to know many new things related to hidden aspects of themselves, but due to a lack of self-experience, they only have a dim idea of reality. It was still difficult for them to grasp the whole concept in one glance. So, least bothering about it, they switched the talks towards their accomplishments and material prosperity to each other. So the discussion took a turn towards normal affairs of life. Ramesh also didn't find it right to interrupt them and also started to partake in the discussion of various life events that have occurred in their lives. Due to so much excitement, they felt after meeting with each other they forgot about the time. After some time, they realised that it had been very late now and they had to return to their homes as their families had been long waiting for them.

a) Goal of life

We become what we think we are. So our destiny is majorly dependent upon our thinking. It has been observed that our whole life is just the crux of our intention. We groom into the personality that we have decided for ourselves. Once we have formed our mental schema, it becomes very difficult to alter it. We only look for clues in our environment that support our cause and remain blindfolded towards other aspects. If we embrace higher ideals in life, then our energy is channelled for higher purposes. However, if we do not commit ourselves to certain higher causes, then our energy remains entangled in lower aspects of life. For living an ideal life, we must create higher values in life. Thus, our life is determined by our value system.

Now somebody says that this is the handy work of the almighty, who takes us to our destiny and directs our way. But if we go deep, then we will realise that cosmic energy is of help to us only when we are ready to move on the righteous path, shedding behind all ignorance and malice. For this, we need to take the first step towards the right direction, based upon our inner voice, as it is we who have ourselves diverted from our goal in the first place. It is pertinent to mention here that the royal way to connect with our inner voice is through regular enchanting of Aum.

People are often seen saying that these are only genes that impact the psyche and personality of the person and thereby decide their destinies. But we should somehow reflect and take a partial deviation from their standpoint. No doubt genes do favour a lot in shaping the destiny of one's life. But these are not the sole parameters for defining the goal of life. What instead also matters is our upbringing, the environment that we are put in, the ideals that we embrace, the blessings we receive from the universe in the form of good deeds, the understanding we create in our life, adhering to the universal laws that sprout in the form of our deeds, both present and past imprints on mind, at the higher realm our surrender to the cosmos, which also attracts universal grace to sprout in, and lastly our intentions, which attract everything that we receive in our life.

One has to understand that a person is not a body of five elements whose destiny is solely dependent upon genotypes, but many forces play a vital role in deciding one's fate. For instance, our level of awareness and consciousness also determines what we would receive in life. This helps us to understand our existence beyond this body, mind, and intellect and helps us to get acquainted with the true purpose of our life. After thorough understanding, we can work upon our bodily components and upon our genes, which can further guide the way of our life.

History is full of such examples, full of those persons who meet their life's purposes despite being put up in awkward circumstances. Their genes did not decide what would happen to them. On the contrary, they channelled and thereby made use of their genes, nourished them regularly, faced the wrath of nature open-handedly, and thus came victorious. Greatness cannot be bestowed upon us by the quality of our genes. History also tells us that great minds are often born in middle-class families and possess fragile bodies. Having been born this way, they get a lot of space to learn while facing the harshness of nature. But they never surrendered to the outside circumstances and were able to discover the light or knowledge within. They thus shun the life of ignorance, thereby challenging their limits and emerging as the winners of their lives. These are only our deeds that turn ordinary human life into a divine one. Nobody can actually realise its being, who works only to meet his selfish ends. We must extend helping hands to those in need. We must enlighten the lives of others and become the spark that guides their way. Indeed, we must belong to this whole universe, whose indivisible part we are.

It is prudent to mention here that everything aroundIt is prudent to mention here that everything around us has its constitution, and its functioning is based upon its nature. We can't readily alter the flow of nature, nor should we try to do. What we should do is carry ourselves in the best way and should try to not create resistance to any aspect of nature. This way, we can create room for proximity with others without compromising our ethos and ethics. It is only our unconditional love and care for others that ultimately unites us to our source.

We are souls who have taken residence in this body. Karmas can impact the body, but one whose mind is always concentrated upon its true nature, i.e., the soul, always remains above this worldly life. Such persons whose bodies are subject to the Karmas but whose minds dwell in the divinity, sooner or later altering the course of their Karmas, become one with the Almighty. They not only realise their vast potential but also express it while living an ordinary life with an extraordinary purpose.